Theory of Knowledge

FOR THE IB DIPLOMA

Sara Santrampurwala

Kosta Lekanides

Adam Rothwell

Jill Rutherford

Roz Trudgon

OXFORD
UNIVERSITY PRESS

Contents

Section 5: Big ideas

A summary of some big ideas and people that have shaped our world. This section will give you a starting point from which you can launch your own

Section 6: TOKOPOLIS – the game of taming TOK

If TOK is too abstract for you, at the end of this book you'll find a TOK

BIG questions

Scattered throughout the book are several big questions and perspectives on the answers to those questions. These pages give you some background on shared knowledge about these questions.

A word on the approach and thanks

The authors of the various parts of this book are representatives of several different cultures. We live on different continents and have had different experiences of life, TOK, and teaching. But we do not start to suggest that the content in this book is fully representative of our multicultural world. We have received an education in the Western and Asian traditions by and large and that has shaped who we are. We hope that we are understanding of others' differences and certainly try to be so but also recognise that our personal experiences lead to particular worldviews.

TOK feeds into every subject and every subject feeds into TOK – it is, in many ways, a never-ending journey. It is not the intention of the authors to cover every perspective nor every WOK and AOK in this short guide. What we are trying to do is to give you a window into TOK and the tools to help you explore it more fully. The skills outlined in this book will be useful in every aspect of the IB Diploma Programme but, naturally, are focussed on the prescribed assessments for the TOK course. These skills will, we hope, enable students to approach the TOK essay and presentation with confidence. The book is also supported by some sample student material, which you will find at www.oxfordsecondary. co.uk/tokskills.

It is only because of the generosity of many colleagues who have contributed ideas and pieces of work that this book has been written. We thank the following in particular, with gratitude: Tom Arbuthnott, Sue Austin, Michael Dunn, Nick Lee, Karla Schmidt, Gautam Sen, and Andrew Watson.

Any omissions and errors are entirely those of the authors named on the cover.

SECTION 1
Introduction

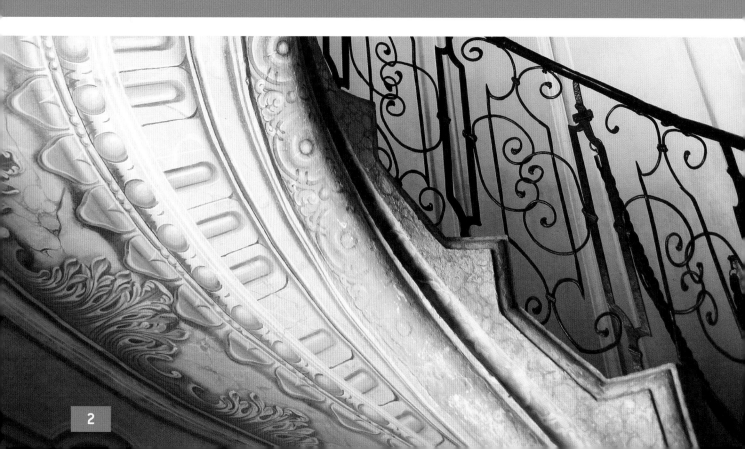

What is this book for?

Theory of knowledge (TOK) is a great subject, but it's one that can feel complicated, or even a bit scary. It doesn't need to be this way – and that's why we've written this book. Provided that you approach it in the right way, TOK can actually be quite straightforward, and once you've got the hang of how to 'think TOK', then it really can improve your life, helping you to think more critically and clearly about the world around you.

The purpose of this book is to show you how to get the most out of TOK. We've cut down on jargon, stripping TOK back to its fascinating essentials. We've also written with assessment in mind: our goal has been to make this book a tool that can help any IB Diploma student (or their teacher) with preparation for the presentation and essay.

who is this book for?

what is TOK about?

what do you have to do for TOK?

why may TOK change the way you think?

The authors of this book are current or former TOK teachers with long experience of how this unique subject can be approached in a variety of schools across the world. We have written in the light of our experience, and we've tested what we've written in our own lessons. We know what works, and what doesn't. Everything in this book could have a place on a well-designed TOK course.

Our experience is practical, and that's why we've written this practical guide: it's what we know the most about. We must also emphasize who we're *not*. We're not IB officials, we didn't write the subject guide, and we didn't invent those famous TOK acronyms. This book is not prescriptive, and you shouldn't think that just because we've included something (or missed something out), then this is a sign that it must (or must not) be taught. However, we have spent a lot of time thinking about the subject guide (first assessment 2015, available in the Online Curriculum Centre) and about how its new features and terms (like knowledge frameworks) could play a part in TOK lessons.

In essence, this is a guide on **'How to think TOK'**.

Who is this book for?

This book is for anyone involved in TOK – students or teachers – who wants a new take on how to approach the subject. We remember how intimidating TOK can feel as a new student (or teacher), and our main aim is to remove this fear for anyone approaching the subject for the first time, or anyone who feels apprehensive about TOK. We want you to approach the two assessment tasks with confidence, and the skills we discuss in the pages of this book should enable you to do just that.

What TOK is

TOK teaches you how to think. You don't have to *know* anything in particular to be good at TOK. Unlike in any other subject there's no list of facts or formulae that you need to memorize. To get a good TOK grade, all you need to do is to show that you are able to think.

Of course, in TOK you need to show you can think in a particular way – there are no marks available for showing that you can complete crosswords in record time, for example, or for showing that you are a whizz at chess. The thinking you learn in TOK is how to analyse tricky questions *about knowledge* – questions that could crop up in any of your other IB Diploma subjects, or even in the real world.

These questions, which could range from something rather abstract like 'How do we know when to trust our intuition?' to the more concrete, like "How do we know when to trust eyewitness accounts of an event?' are at the heart of TOK. They're called **knowledge questions**, and showing that you know how to answer them critically and objectively is the skill which underpins TOK.

TOK students are always asking 'How do you know that?' By the end of your TOK course, you should understand that knowledge is rarely as certain as it first seems, and that we come to know things in a variety of ways – the sheer number of which might surprise you. Answering knowledge questions – a process which always begins with the further question 'How do you know that?' – should turn you into a reflective, analytical student who takes nothing for granted.

What TOK is not

TOK is not philosophy. It is not epistemology even though, for philosophers, this might seem perplexing – and it's different from any other subject taught in school today. It's worth emphasizing again that you don't need to *know* anything in particular to be a good TOK student: all the essay and presentation mark schemes want you to do is to show that you can *think about* knowledge. *What* knowledge you think about, precisely, is not the crucial factor when your TOK essay is marked. TOK is designed to get you to reflect on what you've learned elsewhere.

What's in this book?

Some TOK teachers argue that, because you don't need to know any specific content for TOK, then textbooks are a waste of time. We see what they mean, but we disagree. What we've tried to do with this book is to include pointers that will help you reflect on what you already know, plus lots of advice on getting the highest marks possible in your presentation and for your essay. We have organized this book into the following sections:

Section 2 – TOK terms and skills

This section sets out the fundamentals of TOK – the key terms and how to start thinking about knowledge questions. In other words, this section should give you the tools to 'think TOK'.

Section 3 – Applying TOK skills

Here, we give you some examples of real-life situations that you could think about using the tools provided in Section 2.

Section 4 – Towards assessment

In this section, we look in-depth at the essay and the presentation, guiding you through the sometimes complicated process of using TOK for the work which will contribute to your final mark.

Section 5 – Big ideas

Here we get a bit philosophical, giving you a rundown on what some of the biggest thinkers in history have had to say about the issues TOK students face in every lesson. We've done this because we think it's interesting to see what other people have thought about these questions, not because you need to learn what they had to say!

The big ideas in Section 5 are complemented by the **'Big questions'** that appear throughout the book.

TOKOPOLIS

If TOK still seems a bit abstract, this is a game for you to try. It allows you to take TOK scenarios and to discuss them using physical representations of the terms. It makes TOK less abstract and might help you understand it better.

Colour coding and icons used in this book:

Task	These activities may be for a group or an individual assignment. They will help you put your TOK skills into practice.
Knowledge claim	These are statements that make assertions to truth. Claims that are made about knowledge as opposed to subject-specific content.
Knowledge question	Knowledge questions are questions about the nature of knowledge.
Real-life situation	A contemporary situation or issue which is local and/or global or a personal experience that has the potential to be controversial.
Find out more	Throughout section 5, we include lots of suggestions for further research on websites, in books and other media.
?➡	This icon points out 'Think TOK' questions. These aren't knowledge questions, but you can use them as starting points for class discussion, written tasks, or your own research.

Abbreviations used in this book:

Area of knowledge	AOK
Way of knowing	WOK
Knowledge claim	KC
Knowledge question	KQ
Knowledge framework	KF
Real-life situation	RLS
Theory of knowledge	TOK

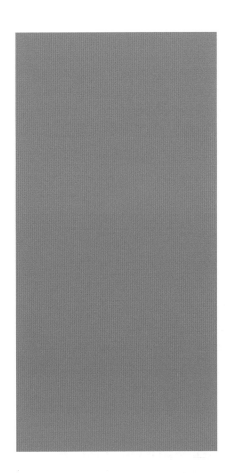

What is knowledge?

Knowledge is something that helps us to make sense of the world around us. In TOK, there are eight types of knowledge or areas of knowledge (AOKs) and each of these helps us to understand a different part of the world.

Each area of knowledge is useful to us in a different way. History, for example, is an area of knowledge that helps us to understand things that happened in the past. Natural science helps us to understand the laws of nature. Ethics helps us to understand tricky questions of right and wrong. And so on.

It's useful to think of each area of knowledge as a map, with each of them giving a different description of the world. Just as we'd use a map of the world if we wanted to sail around the globe, we'd use the 'map' of knowledge provided by maths if we wanted to understand algebra. In the same way, if we wanted to find the right way from one side of town to the other we'd use a town plan, just as if we wanted to understand the paintings of Rembrandt, we'd use the map provided to us by the area of knowledge known as the arts.

This is why we split knowledge up into eight areas in TOK: it would be a waste of time to plot a journey around the world using a map of a small town, so it would be fruitless to try to find out about the Battle of Waterloo of 1815 using the map provided by religious knowledge systems.

▲ Knowledge helps us to navigate and understand the world we live in

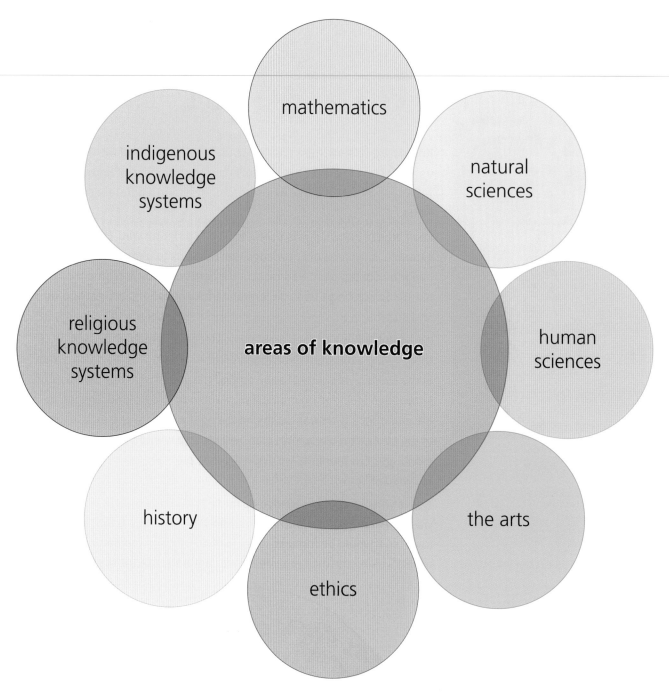

The areas of knowledge

Areas of knowledge (AOKs) are the branches of knowledge, each having its own distinct methods and nature.

For the TOK course, you should study at least six of these eight AOKs:

- mathematics
- the natural sciences
- the human sciences
- the arts
- history
- ethics
- religious knowledge systems
- indigenous knowledge systems.

How to think about the areas of knowledge

There is an IB-approved (and also very useful) way of thinking about each area of knowledge, called the knowledge framework (KF). Each area of knowledge has an 'official' framework that goes with it, and each framework describes how each area can be explored. The idea is that once you have a grasp of the ideas in the framework, you'll be able to ask (and answer) knowledge questions.

We talk about knowledge frameworks in more detail in Section 2, and there's a full description of them in the TOK subject guide, published by the IB.

The language associated with each area of knowledge is a good way to explore it. Here are some terms you might associate with each AOK:

mathematics	axioms conjecture deduction empiricism	logic theorem geometric paradigm proof
ethics	moral reasoning value-judgments moral relativism self-interest theory	empathy values utilitarianism altruism
history	evidence propaganda social bias hindsight	pluralism empathy primary source secondary source
human sciences	observation loaded questions going native anthropology	stream of consciousness reductionism free will determinism
religious knowledge systems	polytheism pantheism scriptures fundamentalism	evangelism religious pluralism secularism monotheism
natural sciences	pseudo-science hypothesis confirmation bias paradigm	relativism theory falsification rationalism
indigenous knowledge systems	tradition culture nomads rituals	folklore storytelling observed phenomena ancestry
the arts	aesthetics kitsch forgery avant-garde	catharsis mimesis beauty contemporary

TASK

Do you recognise all the words in the boxes above? Research any you don't and make a note of their meaning – they might be useful!

Draw a mind-map for each AOK – start with the key terms we've thought of, and add any more you can think of. Do any words appear in more than one mind-map? What does this suggest about the relationship between those AOKs?

You can continue adding to your mind-maps throughout the TOK course, so that you build up a bank of key terminology to use in your essay and presentation.

How do you know?

So far, we've defined what knowledge is, and split it up into eight areas. But that's not the whole story. We also need to work out *how* we know things in each of the areas. In TOK, there are eight 'ways of knowing' (WOKs) – **language, sense perception, emotion, reason, imagination, faith, intuition, and memory** – and each of them plays a role in gaining knowledge in all of the areas of knowledge.

In the past, the ways of knowing were central to TOK, but the IB would now much rather you focus on the areas of knowledge as the foundation of the subject. Although the ways of knowing are still important, their role in the current course is to help you understand the areas of knowledge as described in the knowledge frameworks. You should aim to study at least four ways of knowing during your TOK course.

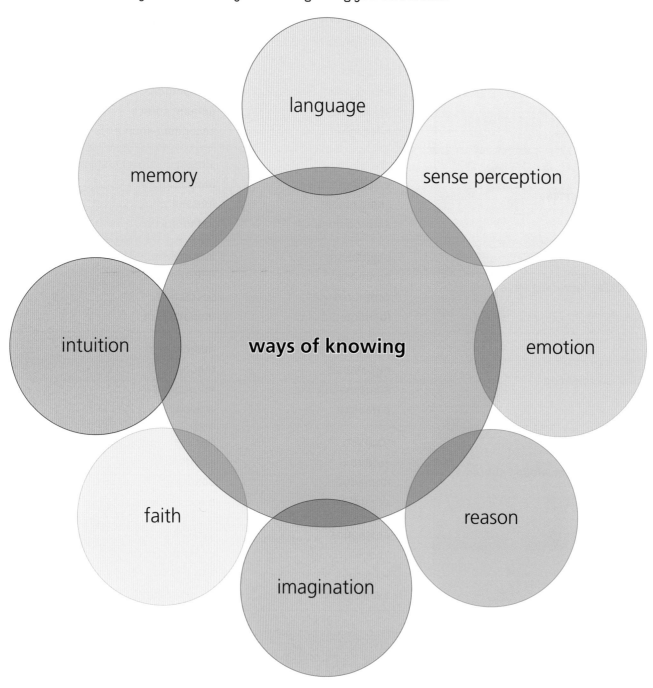

Just as with areas of knowledge, choosing the right language can help you to get to grips with the ways of knowing. Here are some key terms that we've chosen. This isn't an exhaustive list – just some of our thoughts.

emotion	emotional proximity bias emotional blindness romanticism	subjectivity empathy apathy emotive language
memory	eye-witness testimony recall oral memory external memory (devices)	false memories illusion mnemotechnics re-remembering
imagination	creativity surrealism abstractions interpretation	originality re-creating fiction later-thinking
sense perception	realism empiricism sensation scientific realism	illusion fallibility interpretation authority
intuition	cognition inference rational processes instinct	innate knowledge introspection reflex unconscious
reason	rationalism syllogisms fallacies confirmation bias	deduction induction infinite regress vested interests
faith	counter-intuitive wish fulfilment authority paradigms	trust judgement values experience
language	ambiguity denotation linguistic determinism classification	translation communication connotation stereotype

What is knowledge?

Knowledge is like a map—it helps you to understand the world

> Which of the maps on this page is the best? It's an impossible question to answer—each is the best *for its own purpose*.

Knowledge is a bit like this. Like a map, knowledge helps us to understand the world around us and, just as we have different maps to help us to understand different parts of the physical world, we have different types of knowledge to help us to understand the mental world that humanity has created.

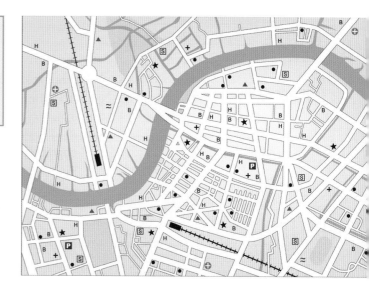

Which map should I use?

If you wanted to find your way from one end of Burkina Faso to the other, you'd use the map of Burkina Faso. If you wanted to find your way around your local town centre, you'd use a map of that town. And if you wanted to plot a round-the-world adventure, you'd need to use the map of the world. In the same way, if you wanted to understand the world of algebra, you'd use the map provided by maths. If you wanted to understand the past, you'd use the map created by history. And if you wanted to understand the issue of euthanasia, you'd use the map created by ethics.

We call the different maps 'areas of knowledge', and you can study each of them using something called the 'knowledge framework'. By the end of the TOK course, you should be able to understand why each map (or area) is different from the other, and what sort of information each map can reveal to us about the world that surrounds us.

How do we know things?

In TOK, there are eight different ways we can know something – eight different *ways of knowing* (WOKs).

Emotion

Although many people think of emotion as an 'unreliable' way of knowing, which is somehow less useful than reason for instance, it's also often the case that we know things emotionally with more certainty than by any other way of knowing. For example, it's usually very hard to reason someone out of being in love, or being very sad.

Memory

Most of what we think we know, we remember. Memory is also vital to our sense of who we are. In other words, it's one of the most important ways of knowing. However, memory can be unreliable, or play tricks on us. Our memories of past experience can also influence how we gain new knowledge using the other ways of knowing.

Sense perception

Without the evidence of our senses we wouldn't even know that the outside world exists. So, sense perception is an absolutely vital way of knowing, covering what we can see, hear, touch, smell, and taste. Although it's vital, people disagree about whether our senses give an *accurate* picture of the outside world or not.

Imagination

It's difficult to define what imagination is precisely, but it's still a very important way we know things. People whose imaginations work in unusual ways are often diagnosed with conditions such as autism or synaesthesia. Imagination is also the key to being creative and solving problems.

Reason

Working things out logically, using reason, lets us go beyond what we've discovered using sense perception. It's a very important way of knowing, but has lots of different meanings depending on who you ask. A mathematician, for example, might see the definition of reason in their subject very differently from a historian.

Intuition

This is sometimes seen as the opposite to reason: the idea that we 'just know' something instinctively strikes some people as illogical or unreliable. However, intuition can be extremely useful to us if we need to make very quick judgments.

Faith

This is probably the most loudly argued over way of knowing. Religious people often believe that faith is the most certain, useful, and important way of knowing there is, while some non-religious people claim the exact opposite, that faith is completely useless. However, we all have faith (or trust) in things we can't know using other ways of knowing, for instance, that the chair you're sitting on won't collapse under you. How reliable is this knowledge?

Language

Language, whether spoken or written, is a vitally important way of communicating knowledge. If it wasn't, then why would you be reading this? But some people would argue that language is even more important than this: that the process of putting our thoughts into words actually *shapes* what we know – in other words, that what we know can be defined by our ability to put it into words.

13

What do I know?

When we say that we 'know something' in maths, that's often not the same as saying we 'know something' in history or in art. Why not? The answer is because these are different **areas of knowledge**. There are eight areas of knowledge in TOK.

Mathematics

Knowledge in mathematics strikes many people as unique: in none of the other areas of knowledge would many people claim that their knowledge is both absolutely certain and able to be shown using rigorous logical proof. Yet this is something mathematicians claim all the time. Are they right? And if they are, what does this tell us about mathematical knowledge, especially when we apply it to the real world?

Ethics

Knowing the difference between right and wrong is something that all societies demand of their members – and people who disagree can often find themselves labelled as criminals. But is ethical knowledge ever absolutely certain? And if it isn't, then does this mean that our strongly-held ethical views should be up for debate? The debatable nature of much ethical knowledge is important to recognize, and vital to understanding human behaviour.

History

Is it possible to talk meaningfully about what *really* happened in the past? Can we know for certain what people were thinking centuries ago? These are some of the big questions that face any student of history, and further questions about the reliability of different types of historical evidence are also important in deciding how reliable and useful knowledge in this area really is.

Human sciences

Human science is *not* science done in laboratories – rather, it's the scientific study of human behaviour and social interaction. Many of the Group 3 Diploma Programme subjects, such as economics or psychology, count as human science: in them, knowledge can be used to draw general rules or principles, but these are often not as useful as knowledge in the natural sciences when it comes to making predictions for the future.

Religious knowledge systems

Knowledge in religious knowledge systems is usually about fundamental and important things: how the world was created, how we should live our lives, and so on. This knowledge is extremely important to very many people, so religious knowledge sometimes needs to be treated sensitively. Religious knowledge might also make claims about a god or gods; but some religious knowledge might not be concerned with gods at all.

Natural sciences

Natural science makes claims about the natural world, and attempts to find laws by which the world works. These laws are defined, often, as the result of experiments or tests, and usually claim to be true at all times, under the same conditions. But how certain is knowledge gained by these methods? And how useful are scientific laws for predicting the future?

▲ Can we ever really know what the Great Wall of China meant to the people who built it?

Indigenous knowledge systems

This area of knowledge explores the ever-changing knowledge of indigenous societies, which may have ancient roots, but are still influenced by recent global developments. Indigenous knowledge may often explain significant natural events, and they may do so using methods very different from other areas of knowledge. You could look at indigenous knowledge systems as a whole, or look at one particular system in depth.

The arts

The arts cover almost everything creative that people do, from dance to sculpture to painting to creative writing (and reading). What counts as knowledge in the arts is often hotly debated, and some would even claim that all knowledge in the arts is personal, rather than shared (and therefore, that artistic knowledge is very difficult or impossible to express). Yet some would also argue that the arts encompass some of humanity's most important thoughts.

▲ Areas of knowledge rarely exist in isolation. The arts, history and religion all feature in this painting.

What TOK can do for you

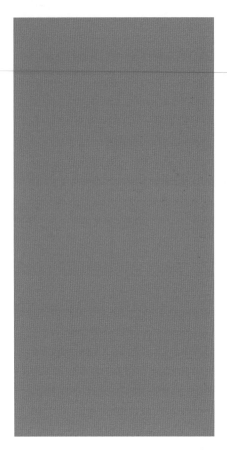

Here are the aims of the TOK course taken from the most recent TOK subject guide.

1. Make connections between a critical approach to the construction of knowledge, the academic disciplines and the wider world.
2. Develop an awareness of how individuals and communities construct knowledge and how this is critically examined.
3. Develop an interest in the diversity and richness of cultural perspectives and an awareness of personal and ideological assumptions.
4. Critically reflect on their own beliefs and assumptions, leading to more thoughtful, responsible and purposeful lives.
5. Understand that knowledge brings responsibility which leads to commitment and action.

From the IB Diploma Programme *Theory of knowledge guide,* 2013.

We can unpick these aims further to discover why and how your way of thinking and approach towards knowledge evolves at multiple levels during the TOK course:

1. Part of the IB mission statement is that you should become a '**lifelong learner**' who helps to '**create a better, more peaceful world**'. Gaining and using knowledge is not only confined to academic subjects or to trying to pass exams, so making connections between academic disciplines and the wider world is what you need to be able to do. Then you recognize that knowing something often brings a responsibility to act as well.

2. We know that for many of you reading this, information on nearly everything is a few mouse clicks or swipes away most of the time. Perhaps more than ever before, we should not unthinkingly accept what we are told, read, hear or see. The glut of information available to us must be examined. Not every idea or fact that comes your way is knowledge. Just because someone thinks it, believes or writes it does not necessarily mean it is knowledge. After taking this course, you should be able to recognize how individuals and communities construct knowledge and be able to examine that knowledge critically. So you develop into a '**thinking, inquiring and open-minded**' person.

3. What is true can be seen from many different perspectives and, if these perspectives are valid and well-founded, we should respect them equally. To be open-minded and caring is an aim of the IB and to understand that '**other people, with their differences, may also be right**' is central to the IB's mission.

4. Knowledge is both personal and shared. You know what you know but there is also much more that you will never know. Knowledge is power so you should learn to use it responsibly by being '**reflective and thoughtful**' and so becoming '**active, compassionate and lifelong learners**'.

5. 'What should I do?' is a question commonly asked in ethics but having knowledge means you also have responsibility to commit to something and to act. Being committed involves being a '**balanced risk-taker**' so also aiming towards '**creating a better world**'.

TASK

Do you recognize the source of the words in bold on page 16? They are taken from the IB mission statement and the IB learner profile.

In a group, discuss these two questions.

1. Do you agree that 'other people, with their differences, can also be right'?

2. How can intercultural understanding and respect help to create a better and more peaceful world?

The TOK guide also includes seven assessment objectives for you to achieve. In the assessment, you will need to demonstrate your ability to do the following:

1. Identify and analyse the various kinds of justifications used to support knowledge claims.

2. Formulate, evaluate and attempt to answer knowledge questions.

3. Examine how academic disciplines/areas of knowledge generate and shape knowledge.

4. Understand the roles played by ways of knowing in the construction of shared and personal knowledge.

5. Explore links between knowledge claims, knowledge questions, ways of knowing and areas of knowledge.

6. Demonstrate an awareness and understanding of different perspectives and be able to relate these to one's own perspective.

7. Explore a real-life/contemporary situation from a TOK perspective in the presentation.

From the IB Diploma Programme *Theory of knowledge guide*, 2013.

These objectives affect your study of TOK in the following ways:

1. **Knowledge claims** (KCs) may or may not stand up to analysis. They may be false claims or prove later to be wrong. So you need to identify the basis of a KC and then analyse that. The justifications of knowledge claims lie in the **ways of knowing** (WOKs).

2. Recognizing and developing **knowledge questions** (KQs) is a key skill in TOK. In the essay, you need to consider the KQ in the title and answer it. In the presentation, you need to explore the KQs that relate to the real-world example you're using in the presentation.

3. In TOK the academic disciplines are known collectively as **areas of knowledge** (AOKs), for example, mathematics and history are different AOKs each with its own methodology (way of working and thinking about the discipline). It is not enough to simply base your essay on your own

personal experiences. You must also consider the **shared knowledge** inherent in the AOK.

4. Some AOKs use certain WOKs more than others. For example, it could be argued that the natural sciences rely more on reason and sense perception than on faith or emotion. Some people are more intuitive or have a more active imagination than others. You need to understand the roles that WOKs play in constructing personal and shared knowledge.

5. **WOKs, AOKs, KCs and KQs** are intimately related so you should demonstrate some understanding of this relationship.

6. In the presentation, you need to present (at least) two perspectives about a **real-life situation** (RLS). One of these could be your own personal experience.

7. The real-life issue or situation for your presentation must be a real and contemporary one, not a hypothetical idea.

What do you have to do for TOK?

TOK is a really exciting subject and, we believe, the more you put in, the more you'll get out. There are no wrong answers in TOK, so don't be afraid to get stuck in! During the TOK course, you need to:

- Participate in your school's TOK classes for 100 hours of class time during your two-year programme.
- Engage in class discussions and stay updated about current events in the world.
- Ask questions in class in order to seek clarity and challenge knowledge claims made.
- Complete any class assignments your TOK teachers set.
- And read, think, and discuss!

TOK assessment

TOK is fairly light on assessment. There are no written, timed exams in TOK.

The IB requirement of the course is that you do a presentation and write an essay. The presentation is about 10 minutes long if completed individually or up to 30 minutes long if done in a group of three. It is assessed by your teachers and moderated by the IB. The essay is no more than 1,600 words long, written in response to one of the six prescribed essay titles that the IB provides and is sent to the IB for marking by examiners.

When you complete these two assessment tasks is up to your school. Usually, you will complete the assessment tasks towards the end of the 100 hours of teaching.

You will be required to complete the two assessment tasks to a minimum standard. You can find out lots more about TOK assessments in section 4.

Task	Length	Who?	Assessed by	Marks	Based on what?
Essay	1,600 words max	Individually	IB examiner Electronically uploaded for assessment	Out of 10	One of the six titles prescribed by the IB
Presentation	10 mins per person (max 30 mins)	Individually or in a group of up to three	Class teacher Moderated by IB examiner You will also need to complete a Presentation Planning Document which is sent electronically to the IB to be moderated.	Out of 10 Each person in a group gains the same mark	Choice of topic is up to the student(s)

The essay and presentation are marked out of 10, with the marks for the essay being doubled at the end to give a grade out of 20. That score is added to your presentation score so the total is out of 30.

That means that the essay is worth two thirds of the marks and the presentation one third.

Both are marked through what the IB calls 'criterion-related assessment'. That means that they are assessed in relation to written descriptions of performance. Examiners do not work through a checklist of criteria when marking essays – they look at each essay in turn and take a holistic approach to marking, with reference to the descriptions in the subject guide. How well other students do is not taken into account. However, in the presentation, if you do this with one or two others, then you all have to be given the same mark.

▲ Not the approach of the IB examiners!

Do I know anything?

The Jain answer: you may well know a *part* of the truth of the world

A famous story from the Jain religion describes the visit of an elephant to a village where six blind men live. None of the men has ever seen an elephant before. The six men each go to examine the elephant, and feels a different part of it.

'The elephant is a pillar,' said the first man who touched his leg.

'Oh, no! It is like a rope,' said the second man who touched the tail.

'Oh, no! It is like a thick branch of a tree,' said the third man who touched the trunk of the elephant.

'It is like a big hand fan' said the fourth man who touched the ear of the elephant.

'It is like a huge wall,' said the fifth man who touched the belly of the elephant.

'It is like a solid pipe,' said the sixth man who touched the tusk of the elephant.

They began to argue about the elephant and every one of them insisted that he was right. It looked like they were getting agitated. A wise man was passing by and he saw this. He stopped and asked them, "What is the matter?" They said, "We cannot agree to what the elephant is like." Each one of them told what he thought the elephant was like. The wise man calmly explained to them, "All of you are right. The reason every one of you is telling it differently because each one of you touched a different part of the elephant. So, actually the elephant has all those features that you said."

衆盲
探象之図

Is this argument convincing? The story of the blind men and the elephant is incredibly popular. You can even buy children's books that contain a version of it, as a way of showing us that we shouldn't be overconfident in our views. But does the story make real philosophical sense? Who, in reality, acts as the 'wise man' of the story? How do we *know* that we're each seeing a part of a greater reality? How could this be proven? And, if we can't *prove* the Jain idea is right, does that mean that the story is useless? Or can we draw other lessons from it?

Jains use this story to illustrate their belief in *Nayavada*—the idea that all views of an argument illustrate a part of the true answer, but not all of it. So even if I hold a completely different view about the world to someone else, we can both still be right, according to this Jain belief: but neither of us will know the *whole* truth.

The elephant story has also been used by other religions, including Buddhism to make a slightly different point: that we can all be wrong without knowing it!

SECTION 2
TOK terms and skills

Introduction: the 'Think TOK' process

TOK teaches you how to think. In TOK lessons, you'll look at the world in a new, critical light which should help you to understand the true value of what you know. This is a big task, and it can seem intimidating. That's why we've devised the Think TOK process, a simple way to see the world like a TOK pro.

Think TOK will help you master the skill that's at the heart of TOK in a straightforward way. Using this model you'll be able to identify what counts as a good real-life situation, and then be able to analyse it using TOK terms and ideas. It's this analysis, and how well you do it, that determines your mark in both the presentation and coursework essay.

In Section 3, we'll show you some examples of good real-life situations that we've analysed using the Think TOK process. Once you've looked at these examples, we hope that you'll be able to apply the process to your own experiences – identifying real-life situations of your own, and then analysing them in the same way.

First, in this section, we explain in more detail what each part of the Think TOK process is, how it works, and how it can help you.

The Think TOK model:

Real-life situation (RLS)

Select an RLS from the media or from your own personal experiences.

Knowledge claims (KCs)

Identify KC(s) made in the RLS. These should relate to knowledge rather than subject content.

Exploration phase

Ways of knowing

Consider the justifications upon which the claims rest. Which way(s) of knowing help create the knowledge claims identified and in what way?

Personal and shared knowledge

What role does personal/shared knowledge play or what implications does it have on our approach to the KCs?

Knowledge framework (AOKs)

A comparative exploration of related AOKs based on their scope, language, historical development and methodology.

Knowledge question (KQ)

Generate KQ(s) from any of the terms or concepts identified in the exploration phase.

Real-life situations

Real-life situations (RLS) or examples play a fundamental role in exploring TOK and illustrating your ideas in the prescribed assessments. If you use real-life examples effectively in your essay and presentation, you should be on track for a good mark.

Identifying a real-life example suitable for TOK is also pretty easy. An interesting reflection on something you have learned in one of your lessons (in any subject) could count as one; so could an interesting news story you have heard.

Anecdotal stories about your pet goldfish or about hypothetical situations, however, won't get you very far. To be really useful for TOK analysis, a real-life situation needs to be something that can be explored and expanded upon by using what you've learned in TOK lessons.

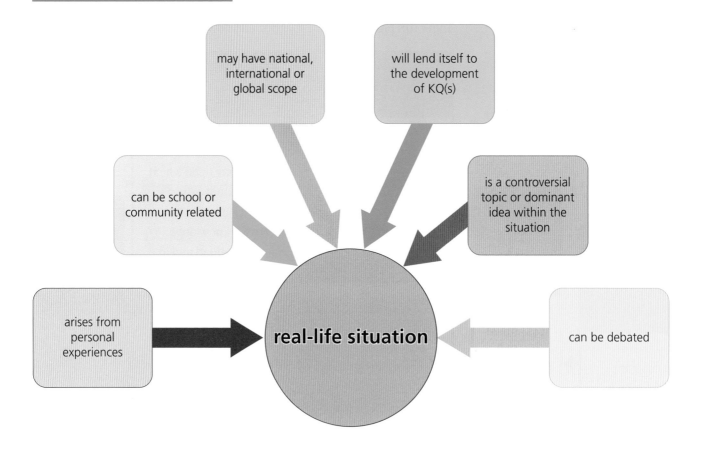

What makes a real-life example suitable for TOK analysis?

- A personal experience related to school, family, religious group, city or country that may have an international or global relevance.
- Main issues or ideas from the real-life example should affect us as individuals or as a society, directly or indirectly.
- The main issues or ideas in the real-life example should be controversial and prompt questions and discussion.

Examples of real-life situations could come from:

- your own personal experience
- classroom discussions from different subject areas
- events or situations taking place at school or in the community
- issues related to your specific cultural context
- lyrics of songs
- excerpts from films or documentaries
- articles
- cartoon strips
- photos
- TED Talks (http://www.ted.com/talks)
- YouTube videos
- advertising or propaganda campaigns
- ongoing socio-political debates related to the implementation of laws or policies in your context.

◀ You might find inspiration for a real-life situation in class...

▶...or at the cinema

On the following pages you will find some examples of real-life situations, using some of the sources listed above.

1. Classroom discussions from different subject areas

In your literature class you are studying the novel 'To Kill a Mockingbird' by Harper Lee. The novel explores the issues of racial discrimination in the USA of the 1930s and it leads to a discussion of racial discrimination in current times.

▲ Scene from the 1962 film showing Atticus Finch defending Tom Robinson from a charge of rape

This discussion could be considered a real-life situation because:

■ it is school-related and has a global relevance

■ the main idea is controversial and debatable

■ the controversial idea may affect us as individuals or as a society.

There are a number of debatable issues in this real-life situation which you could explore in a presentation or essay, including the following.

■ How far has racial discrimination changed or evolved in contemporary times? For example, racial discrimination may not be only experienced by black people today.

■ Will racial discrimination ever disappear?

■ Will we ever achieve equality for all in society?

You must make a clear distinction between discussions that are about content and ones that are related to knowledge (as the TOK course demands).

Here are two examples of how you can make the transition between content based (or subject-specific) discussion to the more relevant TOK ones. You should be able to see the natural progression from the debatable issues in the RLS, through to the knowledge questions.

Content-based discussions/ questions	Transition from content-based discussions to knowledge-based ones	Knowledge-based discussions/ questions
Will racial discrimination ever disappear?	Based on my own personal experiences in my country, I see it as an impossibility.	Is personal experience a reliable source of knowledge?
	Sociology has shown that we are naturally predisposed to categorize people and things and embrace group identity so discrimination is the natural outcome.	Does the evidence of the human sciences offer us concrete knowledge?

Content based discussions/ questions	Transition between content based discussions to knowledge based ones	Knowledge based discussions/ questions
Will we ever achieve equality for all in society?	My experiences from where I work, live or have travelled encourage me to be quite pessimistic about this question.	What role do personal bias and emotion play in defining our perception of reality?
	Established laws in different countries to promote equality in society and work done by international organisations such as the United Nations provide evidence and hope that we may one day achieve equality in society.	How reliable are established laws of a country in affecting a paradigm shift in a society?

TASK

What books and films have you studied in your literature class? Discuss possible real-life situations you could explore.

Any subject could provide the inspiration for a really good RLS. Think about topics you've studied in history, geography or science – can you think of an RLS from every subject you study?

2. Issues related to your specific cultural context

You come from a religious and cultural context where Christmas is celebrated and the tradition of exchanging presents has been an integral part of your family. You have witnessed the competition to buy the most expensive present or the stress that your parents go through because of this additional expense related to the festival. This negative consequence related to a tradition that is supposed to bring joy to the people who practise it presents a conflict.

▲ Christmas shopping in London – a joyous experience?

This issue in your cultural context could be a real-life situation because:

■ it is related to your community

■ it may affect individuals or societies

■ the main idea of the situation is debatable and controversial.

Possible issues to debate in this real-life situation include the following.

■ How far does the media play a role in the commercialization of festivals such as Christmas?

■ To what extent has the giving of gifts during Christmas become a chore or compulsion as opposed to a rewarding experience?

■ Is it necessary to exchange gifts during Christmas to have a complete Christmas experience?

Content-based discussions/ questions	Transition from content-based discussions to knowledge-based ones	Knowledge-based discussions/questions
How far does the media play a role in the commercialization of festivals such as Christmas?	I belong to a very traditional family in which we were clearly taught the difference between the commercial and religious or personal aspect of Christmas. My family is not affected by media projections of Christmas.	Is personal experience a reliable source of knowledge?
	Research and family health studies provide ample evidence to support the commercialization of festivals such as Christmas and the loss of its true essence.	How far does the evidence of the human sciences offer us concrete knowledge?

3. Socio-political issues related to the implementation of laws or policies

 The controversy related to making same-sex marriages legal.

Such an issue is a real-life situation because:

■ it is a decision grounded in politics that eventually has a direct impact on society and the well-being of individuals in that particular context.

■ it is highly debatable and controversial.

Possible debatable issues in this real-life situation include the following.

■ Who has the right to decide what is good or bad for society?

■ How important are the needs of the individual as opposed to those of the society as a whole?

■ What role do religion and indigenous knowledge play in the socio-political decisions made in some contexts?

Content-based discussions/ questions	Transition from content-based discussions to knowledge-based ones	Knowledge-based discussions/ questions
Who has the right to decide what is good or bad for society?	Religious norms and values play an important role in setting moral codes of conduct or distinguishing between what is good or bad for society.	To what extent do faith and emotion play a role in defining moral codes of conduct in a society?
	The way of life that I choose is a highly personal issue and no one has the right to make choices for me in that regard.	How far does the conflict between shared and personal knowledge affect our justification of what constitutes right or wrong?

TASK

In pairs or small groups select one of the forms of real-life situations listed on page 25 and research a topic that falls under that category. For example, you may choose to start with a TED talk on a topic that interests you. Develop a rationale for the RLS you've selected according to the three models we've just looked at.

✔ Such an issue is a real-life situation because ...

✔ Possible debatable issues in this real-life situation are ...

Knowledge claims

In the TOK course, knowledge claims (KCs) are statements that make assertions to truth(s). Any statement made by a person, group, authority, or institution which claims to be true can be viewed as a knowledge claim. TOK, however, is mostly concerned with **claims that are made about knowledge** as opposed to subject-specific content. Claims about knowledge lend themselves to an analytical inquiry about validity, reliability, and certainty. The questions that you would ask in the context of claims that are about knowledge will be related to the methods by which knowledge is generated and the influencing factors related to the acquisition of knowledge.

Consider the following knowledge claims.

Example 1:

> "The law of gravity, which refers to the natural phenomenon experienced by physical bodies which appear to attract to each other, is an established scientific principle."

This is a knowledge claim that is subject related and not about the nature of knowledge produced in the subject. This claim is grounded in science and is established using the method of scientific evidence and investigation.

Example 2:

> "All claims should have scientific evidence for them to be considered as valid."

This is a claim about the nature of knowledge. Such a claim lends itself to an examination of the nature of evidence and its role in producing valid knowledge in science. It is important to note how this claim is not about the subject content of science but about how valid knowledge is produced in science.

The knowledge claim in example 2 is the kind of claim that should be your primary focus in TOK essays and presentations.

Real-life situations and knowledge claims

Identifying knowledge claims in a real-life situation is the foundation on which you will base your analysis for an essay or a presentation. In order to make sure that you have identified the right kind of claims from your real-life situation, consider the following points:

✔ 'What is the main point(s) made in the real-life situation?' This main point(s) should not be a summary of your real-life situation but should encapsulate the overall theme(s) or message(s) that is evident in the real-life situation.

✔ Avoid the temptation to make comments or present arguments related to the subject-specific content in the real-life situation. Simply identify the main ideas that can be extracted from the real-life situation.

✔ Remember you are looking for claims about knowledge.

Example 1

> 🌐 *You read an article discussing the controversy related to internet monitoring services used by US universities.*

The article (*Universities gigged for monitoring athletes' social media use*, Houston Chronicle, 28.01.13) is about a controversy related to the internet monitoring services the University of Texas and Texas Tech University in the USA subscribed to. These universities paid for the services of companies like YouDiligence to monitor the conversations and posts of their athletes on social networking sites. Their rationale for the monitoring was that it was only to protect the reputation of the athletes and by extension also of the institutions. Students and critics deemed this as a breach of privacy and freedom of speech.

Knowledge claims

1. Monitoring of athletes activities on social networking sites is only to protect their reputation and not to restrict their freedom of expression.

2. Information shared on social networking sites has the potential to damage the reputation of individuals or organizations; there is a need to monitor it by subscribing to companies such as YouDiligence.

Both these claims are about knowledge. In the analysis of these claims the nature of evidence available to qualify them as knowledge will need to be considered. Additionally, an investigation into what motivated these claims also would be required. For example, what role did authority and perception play in making claim number 1? A discussion about fact and opinion, and the role of personal and shared knowledge in making claim number 2 would be an appropriate starting point for analysis.

Example 2

 The doomsday frenzy associated with the Mayan and Hopi Mesoamerican Long Count calendar and the speculated apocalypse on 21 December 2012 triggered a lot of debate.

This article from *The Independent* offered a number of explanations and perspectives on the topic.

3 | News

"NASA ITSELF has waged a campaign of facts to combat the fear-mongering, releasing a 6.5-minute YouTube video, in which David Morrison, astronomer and NASA scientist, personally debunked the Doomsday theories. Last month, the space agency published detailed rebuttals of five separate apocalyptic scenarios on its website, including a meteor strike, a solar flare and the so-called polar shift, whereby the Earth's magnetic and rotational poles would reverse, with devastating consequences. While magnetic reversals do take place approximately every 400,000 years, admits NASA, "As far as we know, such a magnetic reversal doesn't cause any harm to life on Earth. Scientists believe a magnetic reversal is very unlikely to happen in the next few millennia."

A few days ago, the Australian Prime Minister, Julia Gillard, tackled the Mayan predictions in a spoof television appearance for the radio station Triple J. Acknowledging that "The end of the world is coming", she grimly intoned, "It turns out the Mayan calendar was true … Whether the final blow comes from flesh-eating zombies, demonic hell beasts or from the total triumph of K-Pop, if you know one thing about me, it's this: I will always fight for you to the very end." Some Australian commentators wondered aloud whether such a light-hearted intervention was becoming of the PM. In Russia, meanwhile, the Minister of Emergency Situations, Vladimir Puchkov, issued a statement insisting that the world would not end this month, a sentiment echoed by senior clerics from the nation's Orthodox Church.

Experts in Mayan culture – which flourished in what is now Central America between AD250 and 900 – have dismissed the doomsayers, claiming the 2012 phenomenon misrepresents the Long Count calendar, and is unsupported by any surviving Mayan texts. The internet, with its capacity for sustaining conspiracy theories, is thought to be to blame.

One such theory is the "Nibiru cataclysm", which posits that the Earth will collide with a planet by that name. The notion originated in the 1990s, with an American woman called Nancy Lieder, who claims she is a "contactee" with an implant in her brain that allows her to communicate with aliens from the Zeta Reticuli star system, 39 light years away. Ms Lieder, who has a website and a Twitter account, says she was chosen to warn mankind of the interplanetary danger that awaits us.

In South and Central America, where the original prophecy was allegedly made, responses are mixed. The mayor of the mountain town San Francisco de Paula, in the far south of Brazil, has urged local residents to stock up on supplies in preparation for the worst. But in Yucatan, Mexico, which still has a large Mayan population, a cultural festival is planned for 21 December. Any British people still concerned about the Long Count's conclusion could perhaps seek refuge in Bugarach, a tiny French village in the Pyrenean foothills, which the web has inexplicably agreed will be spared the ravages of Armageddon – possibly due to a nearby mountain, which resembles the alien landing site from Close Encounters of the Third Kind."

From *Doomsayers await the end of the world – on 21/12/12,* The Independent, 09.12.12

I only had enough room to go up to 2012.

Ha! That'll freak somebody out someday.

Knowledge claims

1. Facts were needed as a justification in order to disprove the speculations.

2. The speculations were unfounded and worthy of mockery.

3. Expert opinion blamed the internet for unduly aggravating the frenzy related to this speculation.

All three claims are about knowledge and the quality of evidence required to justify the information related to the apocalypse as true knowledge. Claim 1 indicates the value of factual information in the process of justifying speculations. Claims 2 and 3 consider speculation to be an invalid source of knowledge and blame the media for misleading people.

You could discuss and analyse the difference between fact and opinion, the value of expert opinion, and the role of media and its influence on what a group collectively considers as knowledge in the context of this real-life situation.

TASK

Work in pairs.

1. Select a real-life situation that you are interested in and, using the model of these examples, extract the knowledge claims from it.

2. Write a short paragraph about the nature of those claims and the kind of analysis to which they lend themselves.

3. Share your work with other students. Discuss the different real-life situations considered and how they have been treated.

Shared and personal knowledge

> Knowledge can be viewed as the production of one or more human beings. It can be the work of a single individual arrived at as a result of a number of factors including the ways of knowing. Such individual knowledge is called **personal knowledge**.
>
> (Theory of knowledge guide, page 16)

TOK is not a philosophy course. This means that you don't need to spend a long time scratching your head, puzzling over what philosophers have said knowledge is. However, it is important to recognize that the quest for an accurate definition of 'knowledge' has always enticed intellectuals and philosophers, making it an ongoing topic of debate. Our aim here is to identify and understand the tools necessary to find out what qualifies as 'knowledge' and apply that understanding during the study of TOK.

Knowledge has many functions. It can:

■ provide a good explanation

■ provide further clarity or understanding about an aspect

■ be used as a basis to make future predictions or generalizations about something in an area of knowledge or about knowledge itself.

Each time you acquire knowledge, it is either from an external source or based on an individual experience.

External sources of knowledge are countless and could include family, education, and religion. These external sources of knowledge are a collective effort of people in a specific field or context to generate knowledge that is collectively accepted and shared by groups. For example, medical science has demonstrated that fresh fruits and vegetables are healthy and it is recommended that people should include a variety of fruit and vegetables in their daily diet.

> ... knowledge can also be the work of a group of people working together either in concert or, more likely, separated by time or geography. Areas of knowledge such as the arts and ethics are of this form. These are examples of **shared knowledge**.
>
> (Theory of knowledge guide, page 16)

Individual or personal knowledge depends on your perception of things around you, your emotional responses to external stimuli and your interpretation of these. For example, although there is an understanding of the health benefits of fruit and vegetables through the knowledge shared from medical science, you may not like the taste of specific fruit and vegetables and not include them in your diet despite their nutritional value.

Knowledge cannot be examined in a vacuum. It is either generated by an individual who has been influenced or affected by varied extrinsic and intrinsic factors or by groups of people who have worked together in a specific context and subject area. In order to define what qualifies as 'knowledge' it is important to appreciate the difference between shared and personal knowledge and examine the different factors that play a role in the generation of knowledge.

Outlined below are key elements of shared and personal knowledge to help you understand what each type of knowledge entails.

Shared knowledge: 'We know because ...'	Personal knowledge: 'I know because ...'
Collective effort to produce knowledge.	Individual experience, reflection and perspective.
Established processes and ideas using specific vocabulary.	External influences such as membership of different groups, for example, cultural, religious, gender-based groups, play a significant role in personal experience.
Easily transferable knowledge due to establised processes.	No established methods for the acquisition of this type of knowledge. Therefore, difficult to teach or transfer this knowledge to others.
Evolves with revolutionary changes in approaches – paradigm shifts.	This knowledge is not static and evolves with an individual's age, experiences, education etc.
Often considered as an authority with regards to knowledge in the related area.	Difficult to generalize as each individual's experience and perspective is different. Personal knowledge also cannot be examined in a vacuum.

TASK

Consider shared and personal knowledge as two circles.

Here are some examples of shared and personal knowledge. Which circle should each one fit in? Do some fit in both circles?

✔ I know that Rihanna is a brilliant singer.

✔ I know that playing my music loudly will annoy my parents.

✔ I know that 12 x 3 is 36.

✔ I know that there are 30 days in June.

✔ I know that Neil Armstrong was the first man on the moon.

✔ I know that the Mona Lisa is a very beautiful painting.

✔ I know that this chocolate cake is the most delicious in the world

✔ I know that regular exercise will help me to stay healthy

✔ I know that Brazil will win the World Cup

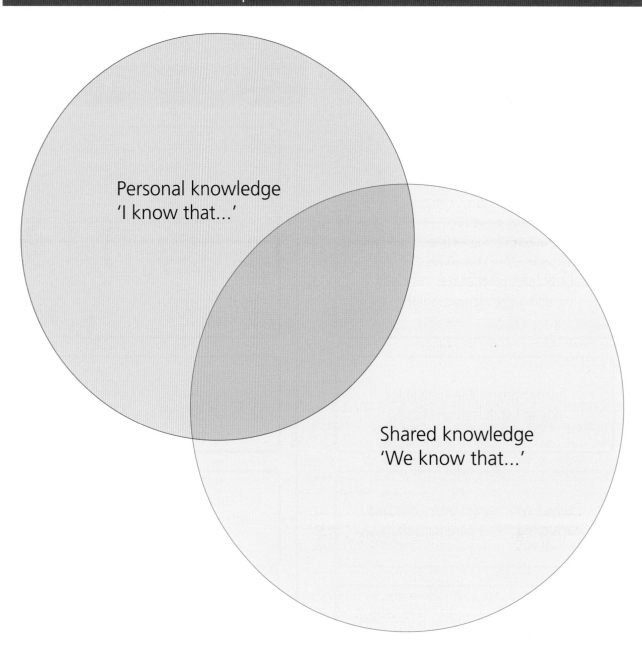

Personal knowledge
'I know that...'

Shared knowledge
'We know that...'

> 🌐 *Maria Callas was an American-born, Greek soprano who is considered as one of the greatest opera singers of the 20th century. She came to be known as 'La Divina' as a result of her musical achievements and successes.*

The real-life situation here is based on a newspaper blogpost about Maria Callas written after her death and a YouTube video of her 1968 BBC interview with Lord Harewood.

Shared knowledge

Maria Callas: the greatest, a blog post by Tim Ashley (http://www.guardian.co.uk/music/musicblog/2007/sep/14/mariacallasthegreatest)

In the post, the writer refers to Callas as the 'greatest soprano of the 20th century', 'unique and revolutionary', 'possessing the greatest range of vocal colour and colossal discography'. Despite the criticism and counterarguments related to Callas' popularity that the writer presents in the article, he concludes with an extremely complimentary comment about Callas: 'Callas' quest to express emotional truth through music has, however, influenced generations of singers and musicians way beyond her chosen field and even beyond opera itself. That is perhaps the most important aspect of her tremendous legacy and the reason why she will always rank among the greatest singers of all time.'

▲ Top of the class – was Maria Callas the world's greatest soprano? Who can make that decision?

The knowledge claims that are evident in this article are:

- Callas is one of the greatest sopranos of the 20th century.
- She possessed a great range of vocal colour.
- She was a great influence on generations of singers.
- She will always rank among the greatest singers of all time.

Evidently these are the views of the writer which may be based on experience, education or media. However it is important to recognize the platform on which these views have been expressed and the impact they might have on a group of people. Claims made by recognized critics of music in established or well-known media (such as *The Guardian* newspaper here) have the potential to become shared knowledge. The music critic and the quality of the newspaper will be perceived as an 'authority' that will generate collective knowledge about Callas and her music.

Personal knowledge

Maria Callas interviewed by Lord Harewood (http://www.youtube.com/watch?v=yM78P3wtqII)

In the 1968 BBC interview with Lord Harewood, Maria Callas talks about her views on music and the rigours of the profession. She talks extensively about her mentor and the skills she acquired from him and how she developed her own style based on that. She also shares her views on her art and opera in general. She particularly refers to the idea of the 'justification of music' and the fact that 'you must serve music'. She talks about finding 'truth' in the music. She continues by saying that opera is old-fashioned music and needs 'some fresh air'. She recommends that lengthy repetitive pieces of music could be shortened and some changes in the performances could be brought about to revive opera.

Knowledge claims in this interview

It is important to learn from a good mentor and develop your style on that foundation.

It is important to be able to 'serve' or be devoted to your art, music in this instance.

Music is about finding 'truth' related to the composer's idea.

Opera music needs a review to make it appealing to a contemporary audience.

These are knowledge claims made by Maria Callas based on her own experience and knowledge. This is her personal knowledge that was generated through her interaction with her mentor and her achievements. The context in which she was performing, the influence of her contemporaries and the nature of opera music in her time all had an impact on her personal knowledge on this topic. In her interview she talks about the importance of costumes and the fact the audience was very much interested in and affected by her costumes along with the music. The fact that she was a woman meant that the costumes, make-up, hair and jewelry played an important role in projecting a particular image to her audience.

Links between shared and personal knowledge

Evidently there are links between shared and personal knowledge. If you consider the claims from the two excerpts, you can see links between the information presented by Tim Ashley and Callas' comments in the interview.

Callas could not simply start singing and perform in a way that she liked without the guidance of her mentor and the appreciation from her audience. The reviews of her performances in the media and the appreciation from the audience gave her affirmation for her personal style and the quality of her art. The recognition of her as La Divina (shared knowledge) provided her with the personal knowledge that she had become successful as an artist.

Balance between shared and personal knowledge

Balance between shared and personal knowledge is extremely important in the quest for truth. Heavy reliance on either will provide flawed perception of information. Considering only Callas' views on her art and her ability to sing does not make it relevant in the context. In order to make her achievements relevant and valuable, there needs to be a shared or collective knowledge of it. Having said that, Callas' achievements and views cannot be considered only through the lens of shared knowledge; it is important to consider her personal experiences and knowledge to arrive at an informed conclusion.

Shared knowledge: Music as an area of knowledge

Music has its own language to facilitate the composition of musical pieces. Callas had mentors from whom she learned some key techniques about music. The directors of productions also played an important role in the nature of her performances.

The audience and their appreciation, reviews in the newspapers, music critics, opinions all affected her popularity and recognition as one of the greatest sopranos of the 20th century.

In her interview with Lord Harewood, Callas speaks highly of her mentor and the different techniques she acquired from him. She talks about details such as gestures and the appreciation of what the composer intended that she was taught to be mindful of. This is an example of how it is possible to teach the major aspects of music.

In the blog the writer suggests that Callas will be an inspiration for generations to come and how her work will always be considered as one of the greatest. However, in the interview she mentions that opera music needs some 'fresh air' and some changes in line with new audiences and a new approach to music. She is alluding to the shared or collective response to music in the modern day, irrespective of her personal opinion.

The accolades and recognition in the media and from established authorities on opera (for example, this article) justified and recognized Callas' achievements and skills. It is the shared knowledge of people that facilitates such judgments.

Personal knowledge: Music as an area of knowledge

Maria Callas' experiences and the teaching of her mentor influenced her and shaped her style. This was unique for her alone. Her views on music developed on that foundation. This is personal knowledge.

The fact that she was a woman soprano had an effect on the kind of costumes, jewelry and make-up she would have which by extension affected her popularity and presence on stage. This experience and the knowledge that comes out of this was unique to her. Also, the opinions of her mentor and contemporaries played a big role in how she perceived her achievements. The context in which she was performing affected her.

Maria Callas' experiences cannot be transferred to an aspiring soprano. One can take her advice and technique on board, however the personal development of a style is very individual, based on inherent artistic abilities. The blog refers to how Callas preferred tragic tones and that was her style; this is an example of personal knowledge based on preference and not taught by someone.

In the interview Callas talks about giving opera music some 'fresh air'. This view is based on her experience and age. After years of performing in operas, her personal view developed into this idea of a review for opera music. Personal knowledge changes with age, individual expereinces, education etc.

It is difficult to generalize personal knowledge. It is important to remember that personal experience does not take place in a vacuum. There are other factors such as time, place, emotions, company etc that affect the nature of the experience. Callas' experiences and her rise to 'La Divina' status is not something that can be applied as a mathematical formula to map out the path to success for a music performer.

TASK

In order to evaluate your understanding of the difference between shared and personal knowledge, complete the following task with a partner.

1. Select an area of knowledge (AOK), for example the natural sciences.
2. Select your real-life situation, for example, the work of a particular scientist, or a scientific invention.
3. Now research a relevant stimulus piece related to your real-life situation that represents shared and personal knowledge separately. For example, an article, video, interview or cartoon for each type of knowledge related to the scientist or the scientific invention.
4. Using the model here as an example, map out the elements of shared and personal knowledge to demonstrate the distinction between the two types of knowledge.

What do I Know?

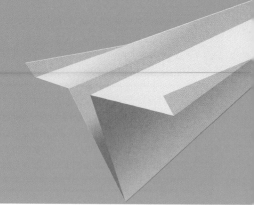

I know some things that other people know

I know how to make a really fantastic paper aeroplane. Given my understanding of the laws of physics, and how lift is generated and drag minimized, I can calculate the best design for my plane, and precisely fold any reasonable-sized piece of paper so it will fly the maximum distance quickly and efficiently.

I know how to do this because I've been studying physics at school for years, and spend some of my spare time adapting my knowledge of physics to my hobby of making paper planes. Using the ideas of physics, I can clearly explain to you why my paper plane design is so amazing.

Shared knowledge

Most of what we learn at school, or as part of any course of study, is shared knowledge. It's usually relatively easy to communicate – although sometimes a specialized vocabulary might be necessary – and can be contributed to by lots of people.

Alice has used the **shared knowledge** of physics to make her paper aeroplane. She's been able to find out what physicists know about why things are aerodynamic and have lift, and has been able to use this knowledge in her plane's construction.

I know some things that are unique to me

I know how to make a really fantastic paper aeroplane. I need to have a piece of paper that's the right size to start with, and then I fold the paper like *this* and like *this* and like *this* – and then a little like *this* and *this*. And then I've made the best paper aeroplane in the world.

I know how to do this because I've been practising for years and years, making tiny improvements to my design each time I start on a new plane. I work by trial and error, and couldn't really explain properly why my design is so amazing.

Personal knowledge

What we know as a result of our own, direct personal experience is personal knowledge. Often, such personal knowledge is hard to communicate properly. What we 'just know' by intuition or emotion is also personal knowledge.

Ben has used his **personal knowledge** to make his plane. He doesn't know *why* his plane works so well, but he knows that it *does* – and he finds his personal knowledge of how to make such an amazing plane very difficult to communicate.

Knowledge frameworks

Each area of knowledge (AOK) has its own knowledge framework – a description of what makes up that AOK. Each knowledge framework contains five key terms which describe a different aspect of the AOK. These key terms, which are the same in each knowledge framework, are:

1. **scope and applications** – what knowledge the AOK maps out, and how it's used

2. **concepts and language** – a description of how the specialist language used in the AOK shapes knowledge in it

3. **methodology** – how knowledge in each AOK is gained, and the processes used in the AOK to gain it

4. **historical development** – how the AOK has developed over time

5. **links with personal knowledge** – how the knowledge in each AOK links with what you know personally, and how personal knowledge can become accepted as a part of the shared knowledge of the AOK.

The official knowledge frameworks are published by the IB in the TOK subject guide, so we're not going to go into them in detail here. However, thinking about the five key terms of the knowledge frameworks can help you to analyse real-life situations in a sophisticated and interesting way.

As you will see on the following pages, using the key terms is a particularly useful way of comparing two AOKs. An essay might ask you to consider and compare two AOKs, and its a great skill to demonstrate in an essay or presentation. The five terms from the knowledge framework provide a good foundation for comparisons.

Let's look at some examples for each of the five key terms. Each example demonstrates how one of the tools could be used to compare two AOKs and the nature of knowledge in those AOKs. These examples show you how to use these tools in your own analysis of a real-life situation.

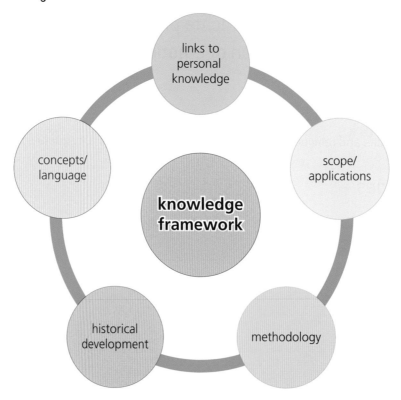

Scope and applications

Mathematics	Art
About quantities, shapes, measurements.	About aesthetic creations and representations of ideas, the physical world etc.
Universal – free of a specific cultural context.	Culture specific and subjective.
In many cultures, mathematical knowledge enjoys a high status in comparison with other AOKs.	Art has the potential to influence societies and promote social issues and change.
A high degree of certainty associated with knowledge in this area.	A degree of subjectivity associated with knowledge in this area.
Mathematical creations have the potential to be considered as artistic and aesthetically appealing products.	Products of artistic creation have the potential to be ugly or unappealing, or offensive to religious or cultural sensitivities .

Concepts and language

Religious knowledge systems	Natural sciences
Special vocabulary to teach principles of religion.	Specific vocabulary to describe scientific processes and discoveries/inventions.
The language of religion could be open to interpretation.	Language used is intended to be functional and free from vagueness in order to ensure clarity of information.
Limitations of language to describe the 'divine'.	Limitations of language to describe new inventions or futuristic ideas.
Metaphors and analogies play an important role in conveying ideas and principles.	Statistics and established theories backed with solid evidence play a big role in conveying ideas and principles.
Transition of scriptures from classical languages to colloquial speech brought about a positive improvement in the appreciation of religious principles and practices.	Language of science has achieved a higher status in the area of knowledge. Anything that needs to be conveyed as valid knowledge may come described as 'scientifically proven' which almost represents a certain authority related to the knowledge.
Specific definitions of what is 'good' and 'bad' offered by religion. Authority imposed by the written scriptures.	Specific criteria for deeming something as true knowledge expressed with vocabulary such as evidence, experiments, triangulation etc.

In both the natural sciences and religious knowledge systems, language is not simply a means of communication but sometimes can prove to be an instrument of shaping a perspective or belief. Additionally, in both AOKs, language also is important for labeling specific concepts and ideas that convey the main content of the subject area.

Methodology

Human sciences	History
Experimental methods employed to investigate human behaviour, for example, questionnaires, surveys, observation of human behaviour and activities, statistical methods etc.	Knowledge in this AOK relies on documents from a specific time period. The main challenge for historians is the selection and interpretation of this documentary evidence in order to present an accurate representation of what might have taken place in the past.
Some assumptions are made of human behaviour and actions or reactions, for example, the ability of human beings to demonstrate rational behaviour or issues related to what is wrong and right in social contexts or the assumption that all humans may consider killing other humans as wrong.	First-hand accounts from people who may have experienced an event or been eyewitnesses are valuable to this AOK but present the challenge and the danger of relying on accounts retold from memory. Individuals' perceptions, emotions, and experiences have an impact on their memory and consequently they may retell accounts in a significantly biased manner.
Application of reason to generate plausible theories consistent with knowledge from other areas of knowledge.	In this AOK the ongoing struggle is to generate a plausible explanation of an available historical source that fits with other established theories.

In human sciences reason and imagination play a key role in the acquisition of knowledge through the analysis and investigation of various assumptions about human behaviour. In history, reason, memory, language, and imagination significantly affect the acquisition of knowledge.

Note the reference to the different ways of knowing (WOKs) in the context of methodology. The WOKs play a significant role in the acquisition of knowledge in the various AOKs and it is important that you are familiar with the relationship between them.

Historical development

Human sciences	Religious knowledge systems
Initial views about human behaviour were based on basic ideas related to simple needs of human beings with specific ideas related to what constitutes right or wrong. Religion and indigenous knowledge also affected these initial perspectives.	Publication of religious texts in vernacular languages influenced the understanding and appreciation of religious principles in a wider population. Preaching in the language of the target audience also raised awareness about religious texts and values.
Adoption of research skills suitable for investigation of human behaviour, such as observation techniques, surveys, statistics etc provided a clearer insight into human behaviour, needs, and actions. Perceptions about people changed over time due to new insights available.	Scientific discoveries and inventions affected religious belief and values, for example, the theory of evolution presented a conflict with religious creationist perspective.
Disciplines such as psychology, sociology, and economics became important and necessary for the understanding of human behaviour. Knowledge from these disciplines has become vital in developing less value-laden perspectives about human behaviour.	Democratic principles of governance brought about a separation of religion and politics. Religion ceased to have influence in key laws and rules of a country. Consequently there was more freedom for people to modify their religious beliefs and create different groups. A clear divide between a liberal and fundamental perspective on religion became evident.

Significant changes and new ideas in one AOK inevitably have an impact on the historical development of other AOKs. The historical development of an AOK is significant to the understanding of its evolution as an established and recognized AOK.

Links with personal knowledge

Ethics	Indigenous knowledge systems
The moral code of conduct in a particular context affects the individual directly. Individual preferences and perspectives may pose a conflict with the established code of conduct.	A large part of this AOK comes from personal knowledge about the self, family history, and culture.
The collective definitions of what constitutes right or wrong, good or bad, has a huge impact on individuals. Individuals may have their own interpretation of what is right or wrong, or good or bad, based on personal experience. These views may differ and present a conflict.	This knowledge is acquired through the narratives and anecdotes of elders and relatives in the family.
Emotion and intuition play a big role in this AOK. However moral judgments are based on more than emotion and intuition. Religion and indigenous knowledge systems may have a significant impact on moral judgments.	Rituals, traditions, and customs play a big role in the collaborative effort of promoting this type of knowledge.

Emotion, intuition, memory, and imagination along with individual experiences, education, and knowledge from other AOKs influence the nature of personal knowledge that is gained. Personal knowledge is influenced by the shared knowledge from the AOKs which has a huge impact on how an individual perceives reality and the world in general. Individuals also contribute to AOKs but their contributions have to go through established processes of validation for them to be considered as 'common' knowledge. The interaction between what 'we know' and what 'I know' is vital in shaping our perspectives and beliefs.

On the following page there is an example of how you could apply the understanding of these five tools of the knowledge framework in your analysis of a real-life situation. Have a good read through the example. The analysis that you will carry out with the help of these five tools is the foundation which will help you to develop in-depth understanding of your real-life situation for the presentation or as an example in your essay. This analysis will also help tremendously in the development of knowledge questions.

Serious claims belong in a serious scientific paper. If you have a serious new claim to make, it should go through scientific publication and peer reivew before you present it to the media

In an online article from *The Guardian*, Ben Goldacre, who writes a column on science-related topics, wrote about an Oxford Professor of Pharmacology who made claims about computer games causing dementia in children without any scientific evidence. Ben Goldacre's main claim in the article is that claims of such a serious nature warrant a scientific investigation or academic paper that is open for debate and discussion. The real-life situation is considered within the AOK of natural sciences.

"I'M ON THE VERGE OF A MAJOR BREAKTHROUGH, BUT I'M ALSO AT THAT POINT WHERE CHEMISTRY LEAVES OFF AND PHYSICS BEGINS, SO I'LL HAVE TO DROP THE WHOLE THING."

3 | News

THIS WEEK BARONESS SUSAN GREENFIELD, professor of pharmacology at Oxford, reportedly announced that computer games could cause dementia in children. This would be very concerning scientific information. But this comes from the opening of a new wing of an expensive boarding school, not an academic conference. Then a spokesperson told a gaming site that's not what she means. Though they didn't say what she does mean. Two months ago the same professor linked internet use with rising autism diagnoses (not for the first time), then pulled back when autism charities and an Oxford professor of psychology raised concerns. Similar claims go back a long way. They seem changeable, but serious. It's with some trepidation that anyone writes about Professor Greenfield's claims. When I raised concerns, she said I was like the epidemiologists who denied that smoking caused cancer. Other critics find themselves derided as sexist. When Professor Dorothy Bishop raised concerns, Professor Greenfield responded, "It's not really for Dorothy to comment on how I run my career."

From *Serious claims belong in a serious scientific paper*, The Guardian, 21.10.11

Scope and applications: Established scientific methods of research produce evidence that is plausible and brings us closer to the truth in the quest for knowledge. Ben Goldacre explains in his article why scientific evidence is important in the context of the claim made by the Oxford professor about computer games: 'Science has authority, not because of white coats, or titles, but because of precision and transparency: you explain your theory, set out your evidence, and reference the studies that support your case. Other scientists can then read it, see if you've fairly represented the evidence, and decide whether the methods of the papers you've cited really do produce results that meaningfully support your hypothesis.'

Historical development: Continuous and consistent use of scientific methods of research has repeatedly provided valuable evidence for substantiating varied claims that were made about the physical world. This has elevated the status of this AOK in terms of the quality of knowledge produced. Based on that premise, the author of this article suggests that the Oxford professor substantiates her claims with an academic paper open to debate.

Methodology: The author is demanding an academic paper to support the claims made by the professor which implies that the professor is being asked to provide scientific evidence acquired through established scientific research methods. The author offers an explanation of what a scientific paper means: 'a scientific paper is the place to clearly describe the gaps in our knowledge, and specify new experiments that might resolve these uncertainties.'

Links with personal knowledge: The author's personal opinion, education, and experience is very evident in the article. Readers with a belief in science and scientific research will agree with this point of view. Young people who are very much into gaming may also reject the views of the professor but for a different personal reason. For the professor's claim to be considered as 'knowledge' which can be shared with all, it will need to go through a validation process established by this AOK.

Concepts and language: Use of terms such as dementia and autism in the claims made in the real-life situation by the Oxford professor sparked a controversy as these are scientific terms and claims made about them are serious which need valid scientific proof.

TASK

In pairs or in groups, select a real-life situation and carry out an analysis like the example here to demonstrate your understanding of the knowledge framework.

Knowledge questions

This section outlines the final part of the Think TOK process considered earlier in this chapter. Knowledge questions are at the heart of TOK and students are required to prepare a presentation and write an essay based on knowledge questions. Before you read any further, go back to the earlier section on knowledge claims (p30) and review the definition of knowledge claims in order to focus on what claims about knowledge mean.

Features of knowledge questions

- They are questions related to the methods and mechanisms by which we acquire knowledge and focus on the ways of knowing used to produce knowledge in an AOK.

  For example: *What role does emotion play in supporting claims made in the natural sciences?*

- They are open questions. There are many possible answers to these questions and there is no 'right' answer for a good question. Sometimes, good knowledge questions may inspire more questions about the same topic indicating different perspectives.

  For example: *On what basis can one theory or explanation about the world be considered better than others?*

- They are general questions. The vocabulary used in knowledge questions should not be subject specific. It should use general TOK concepts to focus on how knowledge is acquired in an AOK. (see page 52)

  A question such as 'What is Newton's law of gravitation?' uses vocabulary specific to natural sciences and would require a scientific response so is evidently not a general question.

  An example of a general question is: *What role do reason and imagination play in generating a hypothesis about scientific processes?*

> Knowledge questions are questions **about** the nature of knowledge.

Here are some examples of questions that could be asked about one particular knowledge claim. Only one meets the criteria we have given for a good knowledge question.

Knowledge claim: There is evidence to indicate that swine flu has become an epidemic.

Question that meets all the criteria for a good knowledge question

How much evidence do scientists need before they accept a theory is true?

An open and general question about certainty and the nature of evidence (TOK concepts) required to justify the knowledge claim made. Whilst the question is based in the area of natural science, it can be discussed with reference to any area of knowledge. This is a good knowledge question that represents all the features discussed on the previous page.

How do we know when to believe something?

Slightly open question that is about the source of knowledge and nature of evidence but it is too general and lacks TOK terms or concepts. Not a good knowledge question but certainly has the potential to be developed further.

Will swine flu kill millions?

A closed question that can be answered with a 'yes' or 'no'. Not a knowledge question.

What do we mean by an epidemic?

Focusing on the term 'epidemic' is a good starting point. However this question is not about knowledge but about the meaning of the word 'epidemic'. Such a question would need a scientific explanation which means that it is grounded in a specific subject. This is not a knowledge question.

Putting a knowledge question together

It is important to look at the different parts that make up a good knowledge question. Question starters like the ones listed in the diagram below make good open questions. These starters are vital in the formation of good knowledge questions. After the question starters, use a combination of one or more central TOK concepts (red box) and/or associated TOK concepts (blue box). You could also add a reference to a way(s) of knowing and/or areas of knowledge if relevant (green box).

The aim is <u>not</u> to use all the elements listed in the red, blue and green boxes from the diagram below but to select a combination of features relevant to the knowledge claims based on your real-life situation. At the bottom of the page, we have listed some of the most common concepts you're likely to encounter on the TOK course.

Good questions starters: 'to what extent...', 'how far...', 'how...', 'what role does...', 'under what circumstances...'

Central TOK concept to be explored such as: justification, validity, bias, reliability, certainty etc. See the box below for a list of TOK concepts.

Associated TOK concept such as: belief, evidence, faith, values, culture etc.

Reference to relevant AOK or WOK

What role do reason and intuition play in the **justification** of ethical values or moral codes?

To what extent can we speak of **certainty** when it comes to claims made in history?

To what extent do the oral narratives of indigenous knowledge systems act as a **valid** means through which human nature can become knowable?

How far is it possible to remain rational (relating to reason) with regards to **faith** and **beliefs**?

Does the subjective nature of **evidence** in the arts make it any less **valid**?

To what extent can imagination be considered a **valid** source for hypotheses?

How far does art influence the **beliefs** of individuals and groups?

Terms and concepts commonly used in the creation of knowledge questions

Expert	Faith	Truth	Validity
Belief	Generalization	Experience	Reliability
Certainty	Authority	Explanation	Subjectivity
Justification	Bias	Interpretation	Objectivity
Concept	Theory	Intuition	Methods
Culture	Evidence	Values	Verification

Unpicking terms and concepts

These TOK terms are useful because they help to steer investigations into clear knowledge areas. By unpacking the associated questions that arise from these terms you can show real depth of understanding of your knowledge questions.

For example, if we take the concept of an **'EXPERT'** we may assume that this is:

An individual who holds appropriate qualifications and experience in a particular field of knowledge. Often they are considered authorities in their fields and as such are believed to be in possession of reliable and useful knowledge.

However, the very same term 'expert' throws up many subsidiary questions relating to knowledge that could be explored:

1. Who determines who is an expert? Is it a collective institution such as a government agency (e.g. Ministry of Education) or an educational institution (e.g. a university) that determines this? What criteria are used to bestow this 'expertise' on an individual?

2. How do labels such as professor or doctor affect how we perceive or accept knowledge claims made by these 'experts'?

3. If I had a passion for football (played the game and knew a lot about players and its history from years of following matches on TV) would I be an expert?

4. How do we reconcile two opposing viewpoints proposed by experts in the natural sciences?

5. What constitutes an expert in ethics? Are their claims as valid as ones made by experts in the natural sciences?

Let's look again at our example from page 49 in order to understand how the parts of the knowledge question come together.

How much evidence do scientists need before they accept a theory is true?

Good starter for an open-ended question.

Reference to an AOK embedded within the reference to expert opinion in that specific AOK which in this context is the natural sciences.

Central TOK concept of certainty. Note that the concept of certainty is implied here rather than explicitly suggested. One needs to be certain before they accept something as the truth. Relevant and satisfactory evidence will lead to certainty.

Associated TOK term that refers to the central TOK concept of certainty relevant in this question. How much evidence do we need to be *certain* about something?

Assessment and knowledge questions

Knowledge questions are at the heart of assessment in TOK, but the essay and presentation take different approaches.

essay focus

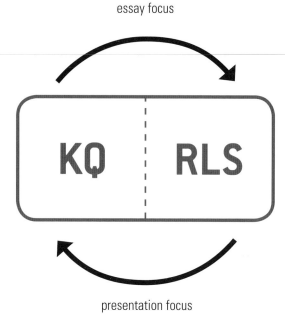

presentation focus

In the TOK presentation:

■ You are expected to identify knowledge questions inherent in the real-life situation of your choice.

■ You should demonstrate TOK analysis of those questions with the help of other relevant real-life situations.

In the TOK essay:

■ You are provided with a prescribed list of six essay titles that are written with general TOK terms and have inherent knowledge questions.

■ You are expected to identify the knowledge questions connected to the selected essay title.

■ You then provide TOK analysis with real-life examples that lend themselves to the exploration of the identified knowledge questions.

Below is an example of how you can take a real-life situation, base a knowledge claim on it, then put together a knowledge question.

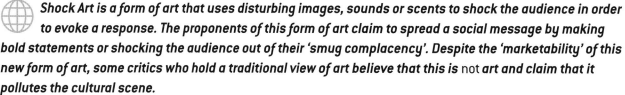

Shock Art is a form of art that uses disturbing images, sounds or scents to shock the audience in order to evoke a response. The proponents of this form of art claim to spread a social message by making bold statements or shocking the audience out of their 'smug complacency'. Despite the 'marketability' of this new form of art, some critics who hold a traditional view of art believe that this is not *art and claim that it pollutes the cultural scene.*

▲ Can a dead shark preserved in formaldehyde be classed as a work of art?

Knowledge claim

> Disturbing images, sounds and scents are considered as art by artists who want to shock the audience with the aim of promoting a social message.

Parts of the knowledge claim:

Central TOK concept – Justification

Possible associated TOK concepts – Expert opinion, bias, belief

WOKs – Emotion, perception

AOKs – Art, ethics, religious knowledge systems

Turning the parts of the knowledge claim into a knowledge question:

To what extent do **expert opinion** and **emotion** play a role in **shaping our perception of what constitutes art?**

Question starter that allows for more than one answer.

Reference to emotion as WOK to consider its role in affecting our opinion on what constitutes art.

Central TOK concept is justification (implied here). What justification do we use to consider something as an artistic creation?

Associated TOK term that refers to the influence 'experts' in art as an AOK have on our opinion on what constitutes art.

TASK

In pairs or groups use the format of the example given here to complete the following tasks.

1 Select a real-life situation.

2 Identify a knowledge claim.

3 Discuss and agree on the parts of the knowledge claim.

4 Form a knowledge question using an appropriate opening phrase and the different parts agreed by your group.

5 Examine your knowledge question in order to demonstrate that it has all the required parts for a good knowledge question.

How do I know things?

Some possible answers ...

1

You know things because you experience them with your senses.

This has been a popular explanation for thousands of years: I know that this desk exists because I can see it and touch it and, therefore, *I know* it's there.

2

You know things because you are in touch with the eternal world – or something like it.

This idea has also been popular for millennia. Ever since Plato in around 450 BC, philosophers have pointed out that there must be something which *makes sense* of our sense experience. Even if I see a desk, how do I know it's actually a desk? And if I see another, quite different desk, how do I know that's the *same sort of thing* as my desk? The answer, according to many, is that you are connected to eternity.

3

You know things because you're able to work them out.

This is another ancient answer, and it's the one the French philosopher Rene Descartes liked in the 1600s: we can work things out in our mind (for example, we can work out that we exist, or that $5-6=-1$) and this is the foundation of our knowledge. We can also work things out from our sense experience, but this is in addition to what we can work out using pure reason.

The flying man

A famous thought from ibn Sina (Avicenna)

Imagine that you are flying – or perhaps floating.

You can't feel anything, or see anything: it's like you're suspended in mid-air by forces you can't sense. Next, imagine that your memory has been wiped by some other mystical force. Now, you should be imagining yourself as a sort of 'pure being' without any sensations or memories of them. If you can think of yourself existing like this, Avicenna has succeeded in making his point: that it is possible to exist – and to know things – without any sense experience at all.

Convinced?

If you are, then you might have to agree with Avicenna's conclusion that it is possible to know things without sense experience. Avicenna's argument is similar to Descartes' in his famous 'cogito ergo sum' thought experiment and has attracted similar criticisms. In particular, we might find what Avicenna asks us to imagine impossible: if you ask me to imagine myself existing without any memories, then what reamins of me? My memories are an important part of me, so to ask me to imagine myself without them is, some would argue, impossible.

ibn Sina, often known as Avicenna, was born in present-day Uzbekistan in around 980. He wrote not only on philosophy, but also astronomy, physics, geology, alchemy, and logic. He died in Persia in 1037.

Why so little Islamic philosophy?

There's not much Islamic philosophy in this book. That's because the majority of Islamic philosophers have concentrated mostly on trying to understand God – rather than answering what we think of as questions in TOK. But three medieval Islamic scholars, al-Farabi, Avicenna, and Averroes are of major importance in any history of world philosophy.

You're a bit like soft wax

Aristotle explains how we know things

The problem

Nothing we see or sense is permanent, yet even though objects are always changing, we still know what they are. A tree loses its leaves, but we still know it's a tree. Our friends and family get older, and their looks change: but we still know who they are. So how do we know for certain that objects – trees, aunts, or anything else – actually exist?

The solution

For Aristotle, objects have properties that we can sense. Things that smell have the property of smelliness. Things that are hard to the touch have the property of hardness. And so on. Our bodies have organs that can pick up these properties: our noses can sense smelliness; our fingers sense hardness. Aristotle argued that our sense organs work by them literally *becoming like* the thing they're sensing. So when we smell a bad smell, something in our noses *takes on the property* of that bad smell, in the same way that a piece of hot wax takes on the property (in this case the shape) of an object that is stamped into it.

Aristotle is traditionally seen, with his immediate predecessor Plato, as the co-founder of Western philosophy. But his writings also had a major influence on Islamic thinking (including the thinking of Avicenna) in the Middle Ages. In this famous picture of the philosophical duo, by Raphael, Aristotle is shown pointing at the ground, indicating his view that our knowledge comes from observations of the outside world.

Seriously?

Aristotle's argument can seem strange at first, but it's been popular with philosophers for almost 2,500 years, and thinkers such as Martha Nussbaum and Hilary Putnam vigorously defended Aristotle's main idea right into the 1990s. But many people, such as Miles Burnyeat, have argued that modern science proves Aristotle wrong: as Burnyeat points out, our eyes don't *literally* turn red when we see something red in fromt of them. But, according to Nussbaum and Putnam, this isn't really Aristotle's point. The argument rumbles on.

How do I know that a tree is a tree?

The problem with Aristotle's idea

In the thirteenth century, the philosopher Henry of Ghent pointed out that Aristotle's 'soft wax' theory did not explain how we actually *understood* the evidence of our senses. Henry argued that even if Aristotle was right, and we were somehow 'impressed' (in a literal way) with the idea of hardness, softness, or, perhaps, 'treeness', Aristotle still needed to explain how we know that a tree really is a tree, and not something else.

Imagine two trees: a deciduous tree with no leaves, and an artificial Christmas tree. They are not very similar at all – one is even made of plastic. However, according to Aristotle, both of them have the property of 'treeness', which is impressed on our senses when we see them. But, Henry asked, how do we come to know *in the first place* what 'the property of treeness' actually is? How do we *know* that the very dissimilar objects above are both trees? Henry's answer was simple: God, through a sort of divine telepathy, tells us that they are.

SECTION 3
Applying TOK skills

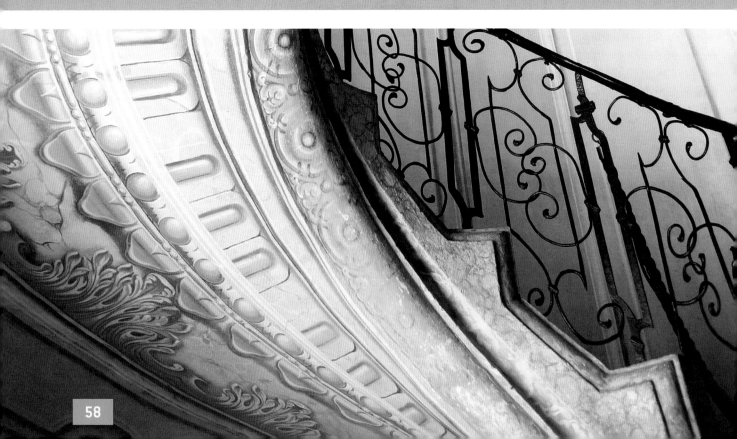

Application of the Think TOK process

In this section, we put together the different parts of the Think TOK process explained in Section 2, showing you how you can use Think TOK to analyse real-life situations in a way which will get you high marks in the presentation and essay.

We've selected some real-life situations that, once analysed using Think TOK, produce some fascinating knowledge questions. As the section unfolds, however, you'll find that we have done less and less analysis: the idea is that by the time you reach the end of the chapter, you should be able to use Think TOK to analyse real-life situations for yourself.

Because we start off with real-life situations, and then use Think TOK to produce knowledge questions, we're doing what you need to do in your presentation: working from real-life situations to knowledge questions. In the essay, you need to do the opposite: you start with a knowledge question (which you'll usually find in the essay title) and then use real-life situations to analyse it. To do this, you can still use the Think TOK process — just the other way around.

Here's a reminder of the Think TOK model:

Exploration phase

Real-life situation
Select an RLS from the media or from your own personal experiences.

Knowledge claims
Identify knowledge claim(s) made in the RLS. These should relate to knowledge rather than subject content.

Ways of knowing
Consider the justifications upon which the claims rest. Which way(s) of knowing help create the knowledge claims identified and in what way?

Personal and shared knowledge
What role does personal/shared knowledge play or what implications does it have on our approach to the KCs?

Knowledge framework (AOKs)
A comparative exploration of related AOKs based on their scope, language, historical development and methodology.

Knowledge question
Generate knowledge question(s) from any of the terms or concepts identified in the exploration phase.

TOPIC: Faith healing

  *Oregon faith healer parents get probation in son's death, Alyssa Newcomb, ABC news, 19.09.12*

MAIN AOK: Religious knowledge systems

RELATED AOKs: Natural sciences, ethics

The "faith healer" parents of an Oregon teenager who died due to a lack of medical care will be required to contact a doctor when any of their other six children are sick for more than one day, according to the terms of their probation. Russel and Brandi Bellew were sentenced to five years of probation on Tuesday after they pleaded guilty to negligent homicide in the death of Brandi's biological son, Austin Sprout, 16. An autopsy found Austin died of an infection caused by a burst appendix.

The couple, along with their six surviving children, belong to the General Assembly and Church of the First Born, which eschews modern medicine. The group takes its belief from a New Testament passage in the Gospel of James that says the sick should be prayed over and anointed with oil, according to Rick Ross, an expert on cults. "They take this verse out of context and take it to mean this is the only thing you can do while sick," Ross said. "In their mind they see it as a choice not between the church and saving the life of their child, they see it as a choice between God and me."

Bob Schrank, an attorney for Brandi Bellew, said despite the couple's beliefs, they are "committed to complying with their conditions of probation." In December, Sprout became ill with cold and flu-like symptoms. Instead of getting him medical attention, the couple chose to pray. Sprout died five days before Christmas. "According to the group and its leaders, if someone goes to the doctor for medical care, they have gone against God," said

Ross. After an autopsy, the Bellews were arrested in February and were barred from speaking to each other since they were co-defendants in the case, Schrank said."[Russel] was allowed to come to the home to visit the kids but [Brandi] couldn't be there. The rule was they couldn't have contact," Schrank said.

Schrank said the Bellews, who did not offer a statement in court, are "great parents" and "at least 20" people sent letters vouching for them. In August, prosecutors met with members of the Bellews' church to discuss state child neglect laws and to let them know choosing not to seek medical care for a child would not be tolerated, the Eugene Register Guard reported. Prosecutor Erik Hasselman told the newspaper congregants seemed to be receptive. "This is not a denomination that feels that its faith is at odds with the laws of the community," he said.

The case is one of many in which parents have been held criminally responsible for neglecting to seek medical attention for their children. Earlier this year, an Oklahoma woman was found guilty of second degree manslaughter and sentenced to two-and-a-half years in prison. Prosecutors said Susan Grady, who belongs to the Church of the First Born, chose to treat her 9-year-old son's diabetes complications with prayer. He died days later. Last year, Dale and Shannon Hickman, an Oregon couple who belonged to the church, were sentenced to 75 months in prison after they failed to seek medical care following the birth of their premature son at home. The baby died nine hours later.

Knowledge claims extracted from real-life situation

- Faith appears to be an unreliable basis for medical treatment.
- Faith acts as a strong justification for action (or inaction).
- The state considers parents who neglect seeking medical attention for their ill children to be criminally responsible. Secular society sees them as having acted unethically.

Ways of knowing

Which way(s) of knowing could these claims find their justification in? Why?

Faith: The couple believes that their faith will cure their child.

Emotion: Their emotional attachment to their faith makes it difficult to accept rival claims.

Reason: Evidence in the form of statistics or registered complaints of negligent parents with the authorities proves that faith is not a solid basis upon which to base medical care.

Intuition: The journalist and wider audience intuitively feel that the Bellews are in the wrong.

Personal and shared knowledge

What role do personal and shared knowledge play? How do they affect the claims made?

Personal: The Bellews' personal experiences of their faith reassured them that they were correct in practicing faith healing.

Shared: Their knowledge is reinforced and supported by the claims made in their religious congregation (Church of the First Born).

Shared: The wider community condemns the Bellews based on its understanding of medicine and/or the ethical obligations of parents.

Knowledge framework (main AOK)

How does the knowledge framework for this AOK help us to analyse the RLS?

Scope: Faith in a particular religion aims to give a sense of purpose and meaning to people's lives. It is taken very seriously in certain communities where it constitutes a bedrock of their identity.

Language: The language of religion tends to be vague, and may contain archaisms which lend it a degree of authority. Scriptural records may add another level of authority.

Historical development: Impact of scientific knowledge on beliefs grounded in religious knowledge. In the context of this real-life situation, the conflict between the church members' religious belief about the healing power of god and the development of medical science.

Methodology: The role faith plays in the rejection of an established and universally accepted authority of medical science.

Links between main AOK and related AOKs

Natural sciences: Inventions and discoveries in the natural sciences that conflict with beliefs and moral codes in religions or with indigenous knowledge systems.

Ethics: There seems to be a conflict between ethical values promoted by religion and those of secular society. In this case, secular society would deem favouring a religious belief over the health of a child to be unethical.

Exploration phase

Knowledge questions

1. What role do reason and intuition play in the rejection or acceptance of ethical values or moral codes?
2. How far is it possible to remain rational with regards to faith and beliefs?

TOPIC: Poetry as history

 According to Homer's Odyssey *and the second book of Virgil's* Aeneid, *the Greek forces which had laid siege to the walls of Troy for over ten years decided upon the stratagem of the Trojan Horse to finally capture the city.*

MAIN AOK: History

RELATED AOKs: Natural sciences, the arts

"After many years have slipped by, the leaders of the Greeks, opposed by the Fates, and damaged by the war, build a horse of mountainous size, through Pallas's divine art, and weave planks of fir over its ribs: they pretend it's a votive offering: this rumour spreads. They secretly hide a picked body of men, chosen by lot, there, in the dark body, filling the belly and the huge cavernous insides with armed warriors."

Virgil's Aeneid, Book II
(trans. A. S. Kline)

Contemporary historians and even a geophysicist have since questioned the truth of the Trojan Horse narrative. The historian Michael Wood, for example, proposed that the Trojan Horse may have actually been a battering ram in the shape of a horse (Michael Wood, *In Search of the Trojan War*, BBC Books, 1985). The geophysicist Amos Nur, after examining the geological evidence of a number of Bronze Age settlements, argued that it was a series of earthquakes that brought down the walls of Bronze Age cities, including Troy (Ellen Licking, 'Earthquakes Toppled Ancient Cities,' *Stanford Report*, November 12, 1997). Dr Elizabeth French of Manchester University, however, argued against any claims that an earthquake may have brought the walls of Troy crushing down as no evidence for it exists on the site currently identified as Troy (http://www.youtube.com/watch?v=W3PonH3Oal8).

Trojan Horse aside, there is even speculation as to the very existence of a war between the Greeks and the Trojans. In spite of the archaeological evidence of a fire ravaging Troy, it is impossible to determine whether it was actually caused by the war mentioned in the Homeric epic. Even Wood himself, in both his book and accompanying TV series, argues that ultimately it is impossible to claim definitively that a war did occur in the first place. We are only left, therefore, with the possibility that it *could* have happened but not the certainty that it did.

So what are historians left with then in their pursuit of truth and accuracy? Perhaps, Michael Wood summed it up best:

"Such ideas agree so well with Homer, but of course they too, in the end are only speculation and I perhaps like all those who examined the question before me have only found what I wanted to find. That has always been the attraction of the search for there can never be a final word on history's greatest riddle, only the perceptions of each generation which reinterprets Homer's tale in the light of its own beliefs and its own needs" (Michael Wood, *In Search of Troy*, BBC TV Series)

Knowledge claims extracted from real-life situation

- Poetry may not be a reliable source of historical evidence.
- Despite the presence of archaeological evidence, it is unlikely we will ever know for certain whether the events described in Homer and Virgil were real.
- Historical writing can be influenced by what the historians want to find and by the context and needs of the society in which they live.

Ways of knowing

Imagination: It could be argued that a large part of history involves 'filling in the gaps' or speculation. The evidence is often linked together by means of what is imagined as feasible rather than what is definitively true.

Memory: What degree of oral poetry is memory recall and how much is imaginative reconstruction? Can memory be deemed a credible source for historical writing?

Emotion: People find it hard to let go of fascinating fictions, even in the face of overwhelming evidence.

Reason: The archaeological evidence can be used to both support and discredit the Homeric story.

Language: Poetry (and poetic license) is often viewed as belonging solely to the realm of fiction which diminishes its degree of objectivity thus making it an unreliable source.

Personal and shared knowledge

Personal: Confirmation bias (finding what we want to find) seems to affect historical writing, particularly when emotions are engaged (for example, a sense of nostalgia).

Shared: Certain stories and narratives are repeated so often by each successive generation that they acquire the status of a truism.

Shared: The archaeological evidence upon which histories are based can often suggest multiple possibilities, making varied interpretations feasible and valid.

Knowledge framework (main AOK)

Scope: History claims to be a discipline that produces an accurate record of the past based on verifiable evidence yet to what extent is this actually true?

Language: What is the difference between 'a' history of something and 'the' history of it? Why has the latter been abandoned in modern historiography? What implications does this have on the discipline as a whole?

Historical development: How much of an effect does the society and time in which the history is written have on the final product? Is history always written by the victors?

Methodology: What constitutes a 'fact' in history? What constitutes reliable evidence? How do historians go about determining the reliability of sources?

Links between main AOK and related AOKs

Natural sciences: Is there speculation in the natural sciences and if so, what is its nature? Does the scientific method preclude or reduce the degree of speculation?

The arts: Is there such a thing as a definitive interpretation of a work of art? Can we ever speak of certainty in art criticism or is this not appropriate to this discipline?

Knowledge questions

1. To what extent can we speak of certainty when it comes to claims made in history?
2. Would the existence of speculation preclude the attainment of knowledge in either history or the natural sciences?

TOPIC: Taboos

  *'"Daring Book for Girls" breaks didgeridoo taboo in Australia', Kathy Marks,* **The Independent,** *03.09.08*

MAIN AOK: Indigenous knowledge systems
RELATED AOKs: Human sciences, natural sciences

An Australian publishing house was forced to apologise today for a book that encourages girls to play the didgeridoo, an instrument that in Aboriginal culture is usually reserved for men. Aboriginal academics accused HarperCollins of "extreme cultural insensitivity" over its decision to include instructions on playing the didgeridoo in an Australian edition of a British bestseller, The Daring Book for Girls.

Traditionally, women do not even handle the long, tubular instrument, which has been part of indigenous culture for thousands of years, and is played at funerals and initiation ceremonies. Some Aboriginal people believe that girls who break the taboo will be infertile. Mark Rose, head of the Victorian Aboriginal Education Association, said that HarperCollins had committed "an extreme faux pas" by publishing a chapter on didgeridoo playing. "I wouldn't let my daughter touch one," he said. "I reckon it's the equivalent of encouraging someone to play with razor blades. I would say pulp it."

In Britain, where the activity manual and its companion volume, The Dangerous Book for Boys, were originally published, both have been bestsellers. In the US, the two books have been on the New York Times bestseller list for months. HarperCollins Australia, which will release its version of the girls' book next month, has replaced some of the original content with material aimed at the local market, such as the rules of netball and instructions on how to surf.

Shona Martyn, the company's publishing director, initially defended the didgeridoo chapter, saying she was not convinced that all Aboriginal people would be offended by it. But today she bowed to pressure, issuing a statement apologising

"unreservedly" for any offence caused, and saying that the chapter would be replaced when the book was reprinted.

Dr Rose, who spoke out after an advance copy of the book was circulated, told ABC radio today that the ignorance of the general public was also to blame. "I would say, from an indigenous perspective, [it was] an extreme mistake, but part of a general ignorance that mainstream Australia has about Aboriginal culture," he said. Dr Rose said that, in indigenous culture, there was "men's business" and "women's business". He said: "The didgeridoo is definitely a men's business ceremonial tool. We know very clearly that there's a range of consequences for a female touching a didgeridoo. Infertility would be the start of it."

His views were echoed by an indigenous author, Anita Heiss, who is chair of the Australian Society of Authors. "I haven't seen the book, but that sort of stuff, had it been written by an indigenous person, or had they actually spoken to an indigenous person … clearly that chapter wouldn't have been in there," she said. "It's cultural ignorance, and it's a slap in the face to indigenous people and to indigenous writers who are actually writing in the field."

The didgeridoo, believed to be the world's oldest wind instrument, is made from tree trunks and branches naturally hollowed out by termites. Traditionally made and played only in northern Australia, it is now found across much of the country, largely because of tourist demand.

While most Aboriginal cultures consider it a man's instrument, not all believe that women should never touch or play it.

Knowledge claims extracted from real-life situation

- The evidence upon which an indigenous belief rests may not cohere with the evidence as presented by the natural sciences.
- There is an assumed truism in the article that cultural insensitivity is unethical and that cultural differences should be respected whatever their nature.

Ways of knowing

Perception: Could you consider this taboo truth or is it just a myth? Would an indigenous Australian agree?

Language: Does the language employed by Dr Rose and others affect the way you view the whole incident?

Language: Does language perfectly explain meaning? Is it clear, for example, what is meant by "men's business" and "women's business"?

Reason: What types of evidence would be required to validate the claims made by advocates of the didgeridoo taboo or to defend the publishers?

Emotion: To what extent does one's emotional proximity to an issue affect their perspective of it?

Personal and shared knowledge

Personal: Personal experience may negate or further reinforce the claims made by indigenous beliefs.

Shared: The collective wisdom of a society can make it difficult to disentangle truth from superstition.

Shared: What constitutes an expert in the field of indigenous knowledge?

Knowledge framework (main AOK)

Scope: Indigenous knowledge helps a society form judgments about its own identity. It is also responsible for shaping roles and responsibilities of members to each other and their surroundings.

Language: Oral narratives (creation stories, fables etc) often form the backbone of indigenous cultures and it is through these that codes of conduct and behaviour are defined. Have indigenous narratives been relegated to the status of fairytales or can they still speak of truths?

Historical development: What role does indigenous knowledge have in a contemporary world? How are concepts such as taboos viewed by modern viewers?

Methodology: Is the transmission of culture through an oral means a reliable source of knowledge? To what extent is an oral testimony a valid means of attaining knowledge?

Links between main AOK and related AOKs

Human sciences: Ethnological narratives (such as creation stories) reflect a society's attempt to explain the world around them and thus forms an integral part of their knowledge. Can human nature become knowable through such narratives?

Natural sciences: The evidence provided by the natural sciences may conflict with the claims made by indigenous knowledge systems. Should they be dismissed outright for not agreeing with the scientific approach?

Knowledge questions

1. To what extent do the oral narratives of indigenous knowledge systems act as a valid means through which human nature can become knowable?
2. How does one differentiate between groundless superstition and authoritative knowledge?

TOPIC: Memory and Food

 Two views on food and memory

MAIN AOK: History
RELATED AOKs: Human sciences, natural sciences

Marcel Proust, that famous Madeleine Cake and Memory

"…and shortly thereafter, mechanically, loaded down by the dreary day and the prospect of a sad tomorrow, I brought to my lips a spoonful of tea into which I had let a piece of madeleine soften. But at the very instant that the mouthful mixed with cake crumbs touched my palate, I shuddered, attentive to the extraordinary thing that was happening in me. A delicious pleasure had invaded me, isolated — no notion of its cause. It immediately rendered all the vicissitudes of life unimportant, life's disasters harmless, its brevity illusory…

…And suddenly the memory appeared to me…But, when nothing remains of a remote past, after the death of beings, after the destruction of things, only smell and flavour, more frail but more lively, more immaterial, more persistent, more faithful, only they last for long, like ghosts, to be recalled, waiting, hoping (on the ruins of all the rest) to carry without bowing, on their almost impalpable droplet, the immense edifice of memory."

M. Proust, Swann's Way, Book I of the cycle 'Remembrance of Things Past' (Lydia Davis's translation)

---

3 | **News**

I HAVE ALWAYS WONDERED why things taste bad to some people. For example, I like the taste of broccoli but my wife can't even swallow it. I can't stand the smell of coffee, she drinks it and loves the taste. What is going on?

How we taste things depends largely on the number and type of taste receptors we are born with, says flavour scientist and chef, Associate Professor Russell Keast from the Area School of Exercise and Nutrition Sciences at Deakin University. These taste receptors are clustered within the taste buds on the tongue and in the upper part of the mouth, and they react specifically to salty, sweet, sour or bitter foods.

"Somebody who's got a lot more receptors for specific chemicals in food will perceive them as being more intense", Keast says. [...] Indeed there's a lot more to explain your personal taste preferences than just your genetic share of taste receptors, says Keast.

"Texture perception and odour perception play a part. Differences in how we perceive the same flavour have a lot to do with experience and what we've been exposed to; for example, many Australians may find certain Chinese dishes unpalatable due to odour differences, but if you grow up and this is part of the food that you eat there's nothing wrong."

A bad food experience can have a lasting psychological effect, he says.

"If you have a dodgy food and all of a sudden you've got upper gastro-intestinal distress and you're vomiting, that can be very powerful in terms of relating it back to the food you've consumed, even hours or days later. If you've had a particularly unpleasant experience it can stay with you for life."

As for the different reactions to coffee, that could also be a case of flavour learning.

"Coffee is a very good example of something that initially may not taste so great, but has wonderful post-ingestive effects. Just as we can have a flavour condition that's aversive, something that makes us sick, something like caffeine makes us feel good, so we like it better. In taste there's an element of genetics and an element of learning."

Why do Some People Hate the Taste of Broccoli?
(http://www.abc.net.au/science/articles/2011/09/21/3321737.htm)

Exploration phase

Knowledge claims extracted from real-life situation

- Memories are shaped by our physical and emotional reaction to food.
- Memories can overpower current experiences and alter the way we 'see' the world around us.
- Emotions seem to warp our ability to recall information accurately, or at least, objectively.

Ways of knowing

Perception: Do we perceive events, people, places in exact detail?

Language: Can language accurately reflect one's memories or does it alter them by adding and subtracting meaning through the words we use?

Imagination: How much of our memory is actually an re-imagining of events? Is memory a creative 'filling of the gaps' or an uninterrupted and accurate archive of our past?

Emotion: Do negatively and positively charged emotional reactions to events and objects distort our memories of them?

Personal and shared knowledge

Personal: Is personal memory a reliable source of information?

Personal: Does the writing of events ensure the accuracy of our memories?

Shared: Is the oral transmission of collective (group) memories a reliable source of information?

Shared: If three people remember an event differently, how do you get to the truth? How does personal knowledge become shared.

Knowledge framework (main AOK)

Scope: Memories often form the foundations of socio-cultural knowledge. These memories help shape a society's identity and that of its individual members. Memories also delineate the way a society record history, often favouring the remembrance of positive traits or accomplishments.

Language: How accurate are historical narratives which were originally written down from memory? Over time, words can carry additional meanings so that the original memory may come to mean new things.

Historical development: With the rise of recording devices, has our ability to remember things accurately been improved to the point where we can speak of absolute certainty of knowledge? What role does memory have in the 21st century?

Methodology: Is the communication of memories through linguistic means reliable? Would a memory painted or recorded on a camera be more useful?

Links between main AOK and related AOKs

Human sciences: The legal systems in many countries favour eyewitness testimony as a reliable source of knowledge. To what extent can we trust eyewitness accounts?

Natural sciences: Is habitual memory (doing things over and over) superior to episodic memory (remembering one-off events)? Is it conceivable that habitual memory reduces one's ability to be creative (that is, you become convinced this is the only way to do things)? What implications does this have in the sciences?

Knowledge questions

1. To what extent does language distort the accuracy of memories and, by extension, the accuracy of knowledge?
2. When can we trust historical accounts that are based on memory recall of events?

TASK

You have now considered four different examples of how the Think TOK model can be applied to build an analysis related to a real-life situation.

On the following pages there are two real-life situations with incomplete boxes for analysis. Copy the flowcharts and have a go at filling the gaps in and developing a complete analysis based on a real-life situation. You may wish to work independently or in pairs.

TOPIC: Genetic engineering and ethics

 The film 'Splice' is about two young scientists who introduce human DNA in their work related to splicing animal genes. What ensues is a sci-fi narrative that exposes the consequences of such research that sometimes could prove to be extremely dangerous. The two scientists create a hybrid with human characteristics and lose track in the monitoring process of this creature. This creature eventually becomes dangerous and its actions lead to events in the narrative that present different ethical dilemmas associated with genetic engineering.

MAIN AOK: Natural sciences

RELATED AOKs: Ethics and religious knowledge systems

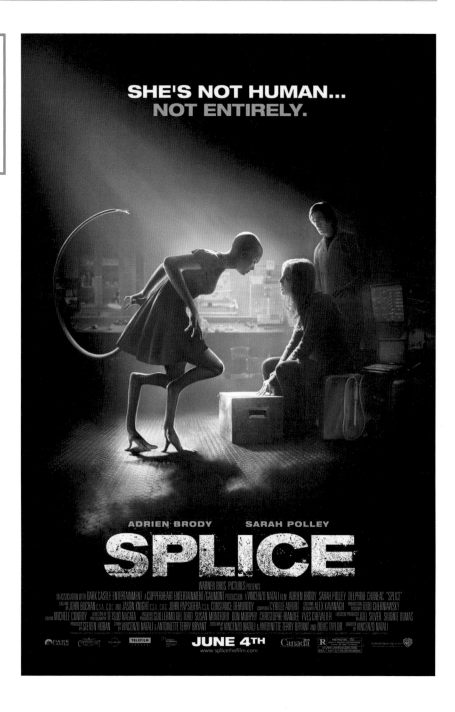

Exploration phase

Knowledge claims extracted from real-life situation

- Scientific experiments could potentially have extremely dangerous outcomes.
- . . . .

Ways of knowing

Which way(s) of knowing could these claims find their justification in? Why?

- **Emotion:** . . . .
. . . .

- **Imagination:** . . . .
. . . .

- **Reason:** . . . .
. . . .

- **Intuition:** Some experiments may seem 'wrong' or 'dangerous' intuitively. How far does intuition play a role in deciding what is wrong or right?

Personal and shared knowledge

What role do personal and shared knowledge play? How do they affect the claims made?

Personal: My religious values help me distinguish scientific experiments as right or wrong.

Personal: . . . .
. . . .

Shared: Should scientific experiments or developments only serve the greater good of people as a collective body or is it acceptable for individuals to pursue scientific experiments for personal gain?

Shared: . . . .
. . . .

Knowledge framework (main AOK)

How does the knowledge framework for this AOK helps us to analyse the RLS?

Scope: Scientific experiments are based on hypotheses and the outcomes can only be speculated on until sufficient evidence for the outcomes becomes available. Consequently, scientists are required to demonstrate responsibility in their choice of experiments and investigations in order to avoided potentially dangerous consequences.

Language: . . . .
. . . .

Historical development: . . . .
. . . .

Methodology: . . . .
. . . .

Links between main AOK and related AOKs

Ethics: . . . . . .

Religious knowledge systems: . . . .

Knowledge questions

1. To what extent do emotion and imagination play a role in concluding that certain quests for knowledge are 'dangerous'?

2. . . . .

TOPIC: Motherhood

 Unique institution offering bachelor's degrees in mothering opens in Ajman, Bassma Al Jandaly, gulfnews.com, 24.03.12

MAIN AOK: Human sciences
RELATED AOKs: Indigenous knowledge systems, ethics

3 | News

AJMAN: Biologically, a woman is known to have become a mother when she gives birth to a child. But this alone does not always make her a strong, caring and good mother. The art and science of mothering is a skill that goes beyond being a gift from life and into the realm of a deep awareness of a child's physical, mental and emotional well-being. By giving her best attention to the child in all these areas, a mother becomes truly great. Experts believe that mothering is a profession and women need to study and learn how to be mothers.

The University College for Mother and Family Science (UCMFS) in Ajman was established to teach women how to become strong, skilled mothers. Accredited and approved by the UAE Ministry of Higher Education, the UCMF offers women a Bachelor Degree in Motherhood and Family Science. Students must complete a four-year course covering various aspects of mothering in order to earn their degree.

The institution aims to make the best mothers possible out of women by educating and teaching them about different issues and subjects — from their rights in international law and Sharia to subjects that include cooking, tailoring, make-up, hair-dressing, pedicures, nursing, breast-feeding, personal grooming and the art of teaching small children and tackling the issues of domestic help.

Origins

The UCMFS was established by the Family Development Foundation based in Al Ain. Dr Nizar Al Ani, Director of the UCMFS told Gulf News that the idea of establishing the university came up in 1999. "We started working on this important project in 1999 and by 2010, our project came to light."

The Ministry of Higher Education has shown a great interest in the project, he added. "Our programmes and topics at the university were studied carefully by the Ministry of Higher Education because they are related to the important field of families and mothering. So it took many years to have our university ready."

Dr Al Ani believes establishing such a university in the region is important due to the many serious issues confronting the society.

"We offer a four-year study programme. We have 137 female students of 14 different nationalities, 80 per cent of who are working mothers," he said.

Dr Al Ani said this is the first educational institution in the world to offer a bachelor's degree in the mother and family area. He believes that being a good mother is not just a gift of nature but also a skill that needs to be studied.

'A healthy family'

"We decided to establish this important university because we have noticed that the divorce rate is very high in the region," said Dr Al Ani. "Also, domestic help problems are on the rise. Eighty per cent of the families in the Gulf area rely on domestic help to raise their children," he added.

There is a minimum of two domestic helpers in the homes of Emirati families, he said. "This reliance [on domestic help] is very dangerous, and there is a need to raise awareness among women on such matters by preparing and educating them on the right ways to raise a healthy family," he said.

The mother and family science holds particular significance in Arab, Gulf and Muslim societies,

Dr Al Ani said, because of the societal changes taking place all over the world which lead to a generation gap. Mothers need to be aware of these changes and gaps in order to effectively bridge them.

One of the unusual things in this batch of students is the enrolment of a mother and daughter duo for the four-year course. "The mother is 44 and her daughter in her twenties and they both want to pursue a degree in mothering and family sciences," said Dr Al Ani.

Course divides into three broad sections

The programmes of UCMFS are accredited by the Ministry of Higher Education.

The course is divided into three sections. The first is about women's civic and legal rights in national and international laws including the human rights of the UN. It is also about women's rights in Sharia.

The second is about family affairs, family health and learning about pharmacy, diseases in the region, cooking courses, home decoration, fitness, personal beauty, fashion and tailoring.

The third focuses on raising children and taking care of them psychologically and physically. In addition, there are courses in computer science.

Any woman with a secondary school qualification is eligible to enrol. All nationalities can enrol. Graduates will be able to work in family courts or other professions that require 'Family Science' consultants. The university also holds all-year-long open continuous classes for women of all nationalities between the ages of 15 to 50 interested in courses such as make-up, hairdressing, tailoring, etc. These open classes do not require women to enrol as students.

Exploration phase

Knowledge claims extracted from real-life situation

- Mothering is an art and science that women need to learn.
- . . . .

Ways of knowing

Which way(s) of knowing could these claims find their justification in? Why?

Perception: In Arabic culture a woman's role in nurturing is considered very important so an educational qualification to promote that role is justified.

Intuition: . . . .
. . . .

Reason: . . . .
. . . .

Personal and shared knowledge

What role do personal and shared knowledge play? How do they affect the claims made?

Personal: As a believer in equal rights and status for women I am offended by the idea an educational institution promotes a formal qualification for mothering and no equivalent qualification for fathering.

Shared: . . . .
. . . .

Knowledge framework (main AOK):

How does the knowledge framework for this AOK helps us to analyse the RLS?

Scope: . . . .
. . . .

Language: . . . .
. . . .

Historical development: . . . .
. . . .

Methodology: Who are the experts on whose opinion this educational programme has been based on? Were they all men? What cultural and educational background did they possess? What kind of bias did the experts bring to this educational programme?

Links between main AOK and related AOKs

Indigenous knowledge systems: The impact of traditional values and perception of gender roles affects the status of men and women in most societies. It is generally difficult to break away from the mould of traditional and cultural systems, however, innovation or change within the parameters of those systems may sometimes prove advantageous.

Ethics: . . . .

Knowledge questions

1. How far do traditional values and education play a role in defining gender roles in societies?

2. . . . .

SECTION 4
Towards assessment

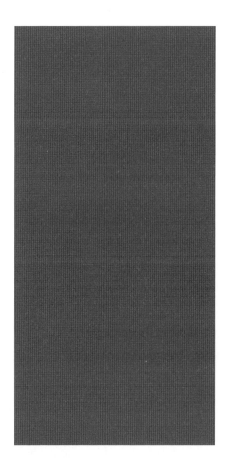

Assessment requirements

TOK is central to the IB philosophy and it's really all about encouraging you to become an inquiring, open-minded learner. However, it is also a compulsory, assessed subject and, as such, contributes to your final grade at the end of the Diploma Programme. All TOK students are all required to:

- submit a 1,600 word (maximum) essay in response to one of the six prescribed essay titles published by the IB
- give a 10-minute presentation (or up to 30-minute presentation for groups of three) on a knowledge question and real-life situation of their own choosing.

Essay titles will be published around six months before the official assessment session. A good understanding of at least four ways of knowing, six areas of knowledge, knowledge frameworks, and the concept of shared and personal knowledge will be required when completing both the essay and presentation.

You are also expected to have a solid grasp of both knowledge claims and knowledge questions (see section 2). The IB's TOK guide contains lots of information on assessment, which you should familiarise yourself with during the course. What we've tried to do in this section, is distil the assessment requirements in a straightforward manner and explain how you can use the skills you've acquired confidently and successfully in the assessment.

A note on academic honesty

Any material that is not your own should be acknowledged in a citation and accompanying bibliography using an approved style (APA, MLA etc). The key is to be consistent with the style used and accurate in the provision of details.

Rightly, the IB is very severe on you if you are academically dishonest. You can read the IB publication *Academic Honesty* for more on this (available in the Online Curriculum Centre).

Referencing (or lack of referencing) is an area where you must be very careful. All too often, students become confused as to when they should cite a piece of work (the common trap of when is information 'common knowledge').

Ultimately, a student will never be penalised for citing information that may not require it but they will most certainly be penalised if they do not cite something that does.

The best way to avoid this is to follow this rule:

When in doubt, cite!

TOK essays

Essay questions

All essay questions (for examinations in 2015 onwards) will be generic in nature and open to inter-disciplinary approaches. This means that you will be able to respond to the questions using a relevant selection of the material covered in classroom sessions.

Past essay questions in TOK have often taken on the form of propositions, asking the candidate to consider the extent to which they agree or disagree.

For example:

1. **'Evidence is always required in order to validate knowledge claims'. Do you agree?**

2. **'Without evidence there can be no certainty'. Do you agree?**

Occasionally, these propositions are quotes based on sayings by specialists in certain fields.

3. **'Extraordinary claims require extraordinary evidence.' (Carl Sagan). To what extent do you agree?**

Another common form of question is one that asks students to consider the implications of a core TOK aspect such as a way of knowing (WOK) or a particular area of knowledge (AOK) that are either specified or left to the candidate to select.

4. **To what extent is evidence always required to support our beliefs in different areas of knowledge?**

5. **To what extent could emotions act as a reliable source of evidence? Consider this in the arts and one other area of knowledge.**

Breaking down knowledge claims

In all cases, a useful starting point is to identify the implications that arise from the knowledge claims made or inferred in the question.

Knowledge claims (KCs) are taken here to mean all statements that make assertions to truth(s).

In essence, any statement made by a person, group, authority, or institution which claims to be true (or correct) can be viewed as a knowledge claim. TOK, however, is mostly concerned with claims that are made *about* knowledge as opposed to subject-specific content (see Section 2).

For our purposes here, let's explore the following knowledge claim made in question 2 above:

> "Without evidence there can be no certainty".

This claim clearly raises questions about knowledge, with a specific focus on the *certainty* of knowledge that can be gained by means of *evidence*.

As with all knowledge claims made in TOK a useful starting point is to ask 'How do we know this to be true?' By doing this, we also imply that we will consider that it may not, in fact, be true or that the claim is at least open to debate.

On the next page you can see how the Think TOK model is used to explore the knowledge claim and its implications through the ways of knowing, the degree of personal and shared knowledge evident and the implications that arise out of relevant areas of knowledge.

Knowledge claim: Without evidence there can be no certainty.

How do we know? (WOK)

Perception: It seems logical to assume that if we wish to be certain we will require a degree of verifiable evidence that appeals, for example, to our senses ('I can see it').

Problems with perception: Is it possible that our senses may deceive us? Is it possible our senses have a limited scope? If so, is it possible our evidence is limited or incomplete? How certain can we be?

Faith: My belief in the existence of a supernatural being may reinforce the certainty of faith-based evidence. My belief alone could be my only evidence.

Problems with faith: One's cultural context or pre-held beliefs may distort the nature of the evidence created making it unreliable.

Personal and shared knowledge

Personal: My memory of an event may disagree with somebody else's. In this instance, how does one arrive at certainty?

Links to other AOKs

The arts: Not all evidence in the arts is based on objective evidence. For example, my subjective feelings towards Lady Gaga's music could constitute an acceptable form of evidence upon which to base my claims regarding the worthiness of her music. This subjective evidence though would not be acceptable in the natural sciences as it does not cohere with their agreed upon method for generating evidence.

Mathematics: When we can observe the real-life application of something claimed, it goes a long way towards validating its truthfulness.

Certain AOKs rely on varied types of evidence. What is acceptable for one may not be for another (for example, myths or emotions as evidence). Therefore, even with evidence, we still may not have certainty as we cannot agree upon what is 'good' evidence (that is, leading to certainty).

Knowledge framework (AOK)

Natural sciences

Methodology: The method employed by the natural sciences (experiment, measurement, repetition, verification etc) helps reinforce the certainty of the claims made. We tend to trust claims reinforced by this method as it tends to offer real-life application to further support its claims.

Data: When there is an overwhelming body of data supporting a claim, we are more likely to believe it is certain (for example, the claim that the earth is spherical).

Real-life application: When we can observe the real-life application of something claimed, it goes a long way towards validating its truthfulness.

This flowchart describes the process you should keep in mind when approaching a TOK essay title.

1. QUESTION THE QUESTION:
In the diagram on p75, the knowledge claim is explored by asking, 'How do we know that evidence produces certainty'?

2. EXPLORE THE JUSTIFICATIONS:
To answer this question, we look at some of the justifications upon which the claim rests (e.g. perception, faith). These are by no means the only possible justifications but rather a useful starting point for further exploration.

3. PROBLEMS WITH JUSTIFICATIONS:
At the same time it is useful to consider some of the problems with these (or other) justifications. For example, it could be conceivable that my personal bias towards an issue may have affected how I chose to interpret the data I collected which could make my evidence distorted or factually inaccurate. Therefore, even with 'evidence' there is no certainty.

4. LINKS AND COMPARISONS TO AOK:
A consideration of the associated implications to the areas of knowledge should also arise from a consideration of both justifications and problems. For example, that the nature of evidence in the natural sciences and arts is of a differing kind thus throwing open the question of certainty.

Developing knowledge questions

Although a TOK essay does *not* require a list or series of knowledge questions to be embedded explicitly, it does help to have relevant knowledge questions in mind when structuring the essay's paragraphs as it makes it easier to focus your attention on one key aspect at a time and helps to avoid descriptive or narrative writing.

By breaking down knowledge claims using the Think TOK model, you will already have a starting point for creating knowledge questions. You can take any of the central terms identified in the exploration phase (in the green boxes on p75) and weave them into a question which invites further exploration into knowledge (usually achieved by extending the inquiry into a WOK or AOK), for example:

Central term to be explored　　　　　　　　**Associated TOK term**

Does the **subjective** nature of evidence in the arts make it any less **valid**?

AOK covered

This question could then be used as the basis for one of you paragraphs.

Visualizing the essay

Once the core knowledge claims in the statement have been evaluated, it is useful to unpack the essay question in a visual manner. This helps track all the relevant points and associated terminology in a manner that can be used to structure an essay's main body with paragraphs that seamlessly link together with ideas flowing from one to the next.

An example can be seen on page 84, where the key term 'evidence' is unpacked by asking relevant **knowledge questions** that arose from the exploration of implied knowledge claims. These are then answered (in the clouds) to indicate a possible line of inquiry that you could pursue in your analysis. Examples, either real-life, personal or hypothetical can then be added to give substance to the flow of ideas.

TASK

The knowledge question above is just one of many questions that could arise from this particular claim.

Use the exploration phase diagram on page 75 to develop more knowledge questions.

How do I know what you mean?

A white horse is not a horse

And in that case, I really have very little idea what you mean at all!

The ancient Chinese philosopher Gongsun Lon (c.325–c.250 BC) once showed 'for certain' that a white horse is not a horse. If Gongsun was right, then it's very difficult to know whether we really understand each other, even when we think we do. This was his argument.

1. When we say 'horse', this word covers horses of all colours and sizes – brown horses, black horses, grey horses, and so on.

2. When we say 'white horse', we are *not* talking about horses of these other colours.

3. But 'horse' *means* horses of *all* colours!

4. So, when we talk about 'white horse', we mean something which *contradicts* the meaning of the word 'horse'.

5. So, a white horse is not a horse.

This argument has puzzled philosophers for a long time. Some, such as Christoph Harbsmeier, have even suggested that the argument is so odd that Gongsun may have been joking. But, given that the argument is actually quite straightforward (once you've got your head around it – it doesn't contain any incomprehensibly long words or strange concepts), the debate it has caused is striking.

You know what I mean

Language is like a game, and we all know the rules

The exceptionally influential twentieth-century philosopher Ludwig Wittgenstein thought that philosophers before him had got it all wrong. In his great work, the *Philosophical Investigations,* Wittgenstein argued that words did not have solid, fixed or permanent meanings, and that, if you thought they did, you would end up in seriously hot water.

Wittgenstein didn't write about Gongsun's non-horse white horse, but if he had, it's a fair bet that he would have said the whole argument was based on a mistake. In Gongsun's view, 'horse' and 'white' have fixed meanings that make 'white horse' (unexpectedly) mean something very different from 'horse'. But this is clearly nonsense. The reason, according to Wittgenstein's logic, is that 'horse' has a different meaning depending on the context in which we use it. *Sometimes*, we use 'horse' to mean *all* horses; *other times*, we use 'horse' to mean a particular horse (for example, 'my horse') or a particular colour of horse (for example, a white horse). In the same way, sometimes I use the word 'game' to describe patience (a card game that has one player), and other times to describe football (a ball game with two teams and, usually, a clear winner at the end of the match). Patience and football have nothing much in common, but I still use the word 'game' to describe them without any trouble, because the word changes its meaning depending on how we use it.

When we have a conversation, we know what the other person means, and if we don't, we can always ask for clarification. And the fact that we are able to hold intelligible conversations is evidence that this system works.

> **'The meaning of a word is its use in the language.'** – Ludwig Wittgenstein, *Philosophical Investigations*

How do I know why things happen?

It might seem obvious but it isn't

How do I know that the sun will rise tomorrow? How do I know that when I take a bite of that tasty-looking apple, it will taste like an apple – and not like a peanut? How do I know that the roof of this building won't suddenly cave in and bury me in a pile of rubble? Generally, we might be tempted to answer 'because it's obvious.' Or, if we're being a little more philosophical, we might say something like, 'The sun has risen every day I can remember, so it's bound to rise again tomorrow.' But neither of these answers really goes far enough. Are we justified in thinking that *just because* the sun has risen every day we can remember, it's bound to do so tomorrow? And if we *don't* believe this, then what can we believe? Anything?

Religions have often claimed to know the answer to this question, whether they answer 'karma' or 'the will of God' in response to the questions above. But this has been hotly disputed, from philosophers like the Scot David Hume (pictured on the right) in the eighteenth century, to the Austrian Sir Karl Popper (pictured on the left) in the twentieth.

The religious answer

Theistic religions (and in particular Christianity, Judaism and Islam) have a very clear view of why things happen: because God – in some way or another – has caused them to happen. Whether it's the creation of the world (shown above in the famous picture by Michelangelo), or anything else, God has willed it, and that's why it happens. Believers in these faiths disagree on the level of control God exerts over individual actions, but they agree that in the end, God's will lies behind the universe and its physical laws.

Indian religions (including Hinduism, Buddhism, Jainism and Sikhism) have a different answer: karma. According to these faiths, all living beings are caught up in the cycle of Samsāra. In the Samsāra cycle, we are all born, live, die, and are then reborn forever, until, that is, we are able to escape by being particularly religious (for example, attaining Nirvana through meditation in Theravada Buddhism). Our rebirths are controlled by the unchanging and eternal laws of karma, which decide what we are reborn as – whether it's animal. human, or god. No god or thing has instituted the laws of Samsāra and karma: they just *exist*, and govern every aspect of our lives. Together, they explain why things happen in the way that they do.

David Hume 'proves' that we can't explain why things happen

'If we believe that fire warms, or water refreshes, 'tis only because it costs us too much pains to think otherwise.'

If you told David Hume that you *knew* why something happens, for example, that a lit match sets combustible materials on fire, he would very probably ask you a question in return: What's your evidence? And it's this simple question that lies behind Hume's argument against causation. In his *Enquiry Concerning Human Understanding*, published in 1748, Hume pointed out that, for any thing which we say causes another (apart from in mathematical theorems), we have no evidence to *prove* the link between cause and effect. Just because something has happened a lot of times before (for instance, you've used matches hundreds of times to light fires), this does not mean that the same thing will definitely happen again the next time you light a match. In other words, there is *never* any evidence that just because something has happened before, this means it will happen again.

Can Hume *ever* be proved wrong?

Ever since Hume's argument came to light, philosophers have been arguing about why his views on causation simply *must* be wrong. The only problem is that nobody has been able to show that he *was* wrong. The nearest philosophers have come is to argue that Hume either missed the point, or else takes philosophy to the point of lunacy.

Bertrand Russell certainly couldn't prove Hume wrong. But he did point out that, if you believe Hume's argument, 'there is no intellectual difference between sanity and insanity. The lunatic who believes he is a poached egg must be condemned solely on the ground that he is in a minority.' Why? Russell argued that if you can't even say for certain that the sun will rise tomorrow, then you have no way of knowing anything *at all*. The idea of what is reasonable and what is not, in other words, evaporates. According to Russell, Hume has come up with 'a self-refutation of rationality'.

You don't *need* to know why things absolutely, for 100% certain, happen

Hume missed the point

Karl Popper, an influential Austrian-born philosopher of science, argued that we shouldn't get so concerned about precisely why things happen. Looking at how scientists conduct experiments, he noted that the whole *point* of many experiments is to prove wrong things we thought we knew 'for certain' in the past. Popper argued that no committed scientist ever seriously argues that they know anything beyond all doubt: everything is always provisional; another experiment could come along and prove everything they thought they knew to be wrong.

So, because no scientist ever says *for certain* why anything happens, Hume's argument is irrelevant. All scientists do is 'conjecture' certain things, which we believe for a little while, until someone else come along and proves them wrong – and, when that happens, our knowledge increases a little bit more. According to Popper, the state of our knowledge is improving all the time, through what he called 'conjecture and refutation'.

Oh really?

Imre Lakatos, a Hungarian philosopher, agreed with Popper – but only up to a point. Lakatos pointed out that if we believe Popper then we have a problem: we have no way of *knowing* whether we are getting any closer to the truth with every 'conjecture' that we 'refute' – all we know is that we are *having new ideas*. For Lakatos, this isn't a problem: in fact he argued that the only way we could know whether science was successful was whether it produced new and interesting ideas. Lakatos argued that, if we can't prove anything for certain – something that Popper accepted – then we have no way of knowing whether we are getting closer to the truth, or not.

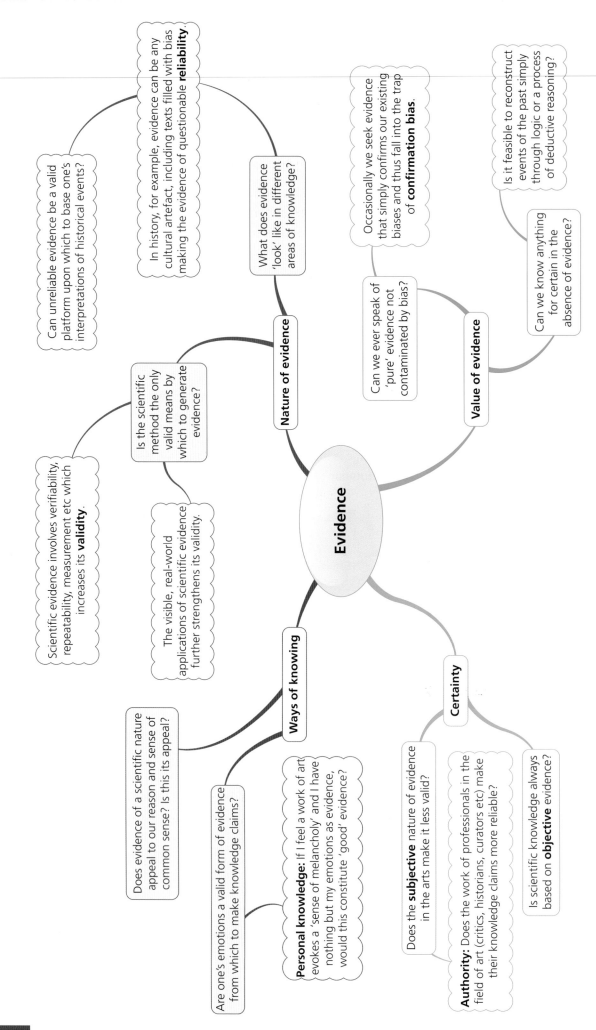

Can unreliable evidence be a valid platform upon which to base one's interpretations of historical events?

In history, for example, evidence can be any cultural artefact, including texts filled with bias making the evidence of questionable **reliability**.

What does evidence 'look' like in different areas of knowledge?

Occasionally we seek evidence that simply confirms our existing biases and thus fall into the trap of **confirmation bias**.

Is it feasible to reconstruct events of the past simply through logic or a process of deductive reasoning?

Can we know anything for certain in the absence of evidence?

Nature of evidence

Can we ever speak of 'pure' evidence not contaminated by bias?

Value of evidence

Scientific evidence involves verifiability, repeatability, measurement etc which increases its **validity**.

Is the scientific method the only valid means by which to generate evidence?

The visible, real-world applications of scientific evidence further strengthens its validity.

Evidence

Does evidence of a scientific nature appeal to our reason and sense of common sense? Is this its appeal?

Ways of knowing

Certainty

Are one's emotions a valid form of evidence from which to make knowledge claims?

Personal knowledge: If I feel a work of art evokes a 'sense of melancholy' and I have nothing but my emotions as evidence, would this constitute 'good' evidence?

Does the **subjective** nature of evidence in the arts make it less valid?

Authority: Does the work of professionals in the field of art (critics, historians, curators etc) make their knowledge claims more reliable?

Is scientific knowledge always based on **objective** evidence?

Paragraph structure

Once you've chosen an essay question, and after you've spent some time collecting ideas, unpacking knowledge claims and considering knowledge questions, you need to spend some time planning the structure of your essay. Your TOK essay must a have a clear overall structure which unites the varied threads to give a focused response to the essay question.

By creating a mind map like the one on page 84, it should be easier to structure the essay itself. Ideally, each paragraph should address one key thesis or line of inquiry that you've identified.

To break it down further:

■ Each element from the mind map could become a paragraph within the essay.

■ Each paragraph needs to be carefully structured and linked back to the central knowledge question in the essay title.

To ensure that you make the most of the ideas you've had, it is a good idea to follow a framework for paragraph structuring. This should ensure that the essay flows naturally and each paragraph has a clear link back to the main essay question. A structured approach to paragraph writing could look like this:

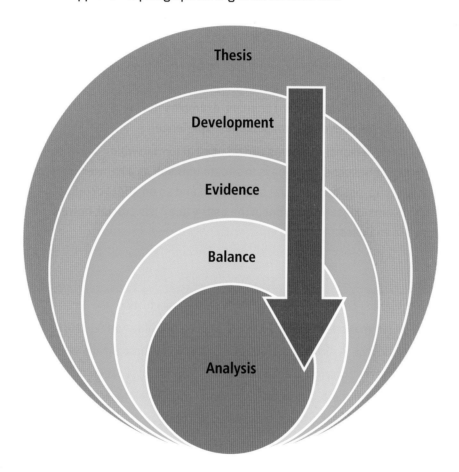

THESIS

■ The thesis is a brief opening line (or two) establishing the key element to be covered in the paragraph.

■ The knowledge questions identified in the mind map should act as solid starting points.

■ You could conceivably begin your essay by agreeing with the claim(s) made in the proposition and then exploring alternative approaches in subsequent paragraphs.

> **EXAMPLE:**
> 'On the face of it, the scientific method used in the natural sciences is closely associated in our minds with the provision of concrete, air-tight evidence upon which to base knowledge claims concerning almost everything.'

DEVELOPMENT

- Development is an elaboration of your principal thesis. What is meant by it? What areas does it touch upon?
- It should flow naturally from the thesis.
- It can offer mini-analyses as you wrestle with the implications of what you're saying.

EXAMPLE:

'This would seem to be the case for a number of reasons, most notably the fact that evidence in science is generated through measurable, cross-verifiable and repeatable experimentation which increases the reliability factor significantly due to its adherence to an agreed-upon method that seemingly provides definitive proofs. This is compounded by the real-life applications that flow from claims made by science which are based upon this method and are subsequently apparent for all to see.'

EVIDENCE

- Evidence is the most important part of each paragraph. All theses and points raised in your development should be supported by evidence.
- This could come from: quotes from secondary sources, examples from real-life situations (news reports, articles, events etc), examples or events from personal experience.

NOTE: TOK is a subject in which personal examples can be used in formal writing. It is most useful when trying to validate or explore knowledge questions. The idea is to situate yourself as a knower in the context of the question. How does your age, social group, position, cultural background and so on affect or influence your position with regards to the knowledge claims/question inherent in the essay title? It is crucial, however, to avoid simple narratives or over-simplistic analyses.

EXAMPLE:

'The very fact that my computer's hard drive is saving information as I type is based upon the principles of electromagnetism which I can see applied and functioning exactly as claimed by scientists. The evidence is directly in front of me validating those claims while my senses can't but go along in merry agreement. Collectively, the real-life application of scientific claims and my sensual coherence with those claims act to reinforce the certainty factor whenever I consider claims that have emerged out of the field of the natural sciences.'

BALANCE

- Attempts should be made in either the existing paragraph or in a completely new one to offer alternative perspectives to the key thesis under consideration.

EXAMPLE:

'In the current example we are looking at the strengths of scientific claims which rest on evidence processed though what is known as the scientific method so it is feasible to explore whether this same method (or model) of evidence should be applied to other areas of knowledge (ie. the arts). Do we always need evidence that is 'objective' to be certain about things? In art, can I rely on my personal emotions as evidence for what a painting by Van Gogh signifies? Is subjective evidence always unreliable? Just because I can't measure it, or cross-verify it or because somebody else may not arrive at the same interpretation as I, does it invalidate my claim simply because my evidence is wholly subjective? Can we argue that the nature of evidence is different in the varied AOKs? We could then consider the inherent bias that evidence in the sciences creates in us and how the same type is not perhaps required in other areas.'

ANALYSIS

- At the end of each paragraph there should be a line or two linking the information back to the essay question you are answering.
- You should be able to answer the following question in each paragraph:

  What insight does this paragraph offer to the overall question?

- It could also suggest any contradictions/unresolved issues.

EXAMPLE:
'Despite the fact that evidence in the sciences lend this field an air of seeming superiority when it comes to claims made, it is conceivable, as seen in example X, to claim that...'

Essay success

The highest scoring essays demonstrate a strong focus on relevant knowledge questions and make good use of all the skills you should have developed throughout the course – acknowledging and interpreting differing perspectives, whilst recognizing the influence of a number of AOKs and WOKs. We've looked carefully at the guidance provided by the IB (which is all available on the Online Curriculum Centre) and have devised the checklist on the next page. Working through this list, both as you write your essay and once you have finished it, should ensure that your essay is on track for a high mark.

How your essay is marked:

- Out of 10 marks (worth 67% of the total mark for TOK)
- By trained IB examiners
- By secure e-marking online – so the examiner does not know who you are or in which school you have been studying
- Using achievement level descriptors, so not comparing your work to that of any other student but only against the descriptors (the official versions can be found on page 62 of the TOK guide)
- By holistic (global) impression marking, meaning that the examiner makes judgements about your essay based on its individual characteristics in relation to the descriptors in the TOK guide.

Essay checklist

The basics:

✔ Choose the right title for you – is it one you are interested in and can write about?

✔ Do not alter the essay title in any way. The IB will provide a choice of six essay titles, from which you should choose one. You must answer the exact question supplied by the IB – you will lose marks if your essay loses focus

✔ Make sure that you essay has a clear structure, with paragraphs which flow in a logical sequence

✔ Present your essay in word-processed format, using a simple, clear font (such as Times New Roman or Ariel), in size 12

✔ Your essay must be double-spaced, to allow the examiner room to write comments as he/she reads and marks it

✔ The maximum word-count for the essay is 1600 words – if you are really struggling to reach this and have to bulk out the essay with superfluous words, perhaps something has gone wrong

✔ If you go over this amount, anything after the 1600th word may be ignored, and won't count towards your mark. You will also automatically lose 1 mark

✔ The word count includes any quotations within the essay, but does not include footnotes, bibliography and acknowledgements

✔ You will be required to indicate the final word count when you submit your essay.

Check that you have:

✔ Written a clear introduction which immediately engages with the essay title

✔ Maintained your focus on the essay title throughout your writing. Is each paragraph relevant to the central question? Is it clear *why* it is relevant?

✔ Identified and acknowledged knowledge questions that are implied by and connected to the essay title. These questions should be at the heart of your essay.

✔ Considered the knowledge questions in the context of different AOKs and WOKs. Include comparisons which demonstrate your understanding of differences between AOKs/WOKs.

✔ Carefully considered the knowledge question(s) from all sides, with extensive use of claims *and* counter-claims.

✔ Supported your argument with well-chosen real-life situations.

✔ Examined the positive and negative implications of your argument.

✔ Made sure that your real-life situations are drawn from both your own personal experience and from the shared experiences of others.

✔ Recognised your own personal perspective, with reference to alternative perspectives

Check that you have not:

✔ Defined terms using a dictionary. Instead, you must interpret them with reference to the title and your arguments

✔ Spent too long describing situations or narrating events. The focus of the essay needs to be analysis. If, as you read your essay, your find long narrative or descriptive passages, go back and edit it.

✔ Made up your real-life situations, or used very common examples

✔ Made general statements such as 'Everyone knows…', 'We all believe that…'

✔ Used other people's ideas without crediting them

TOK presentations

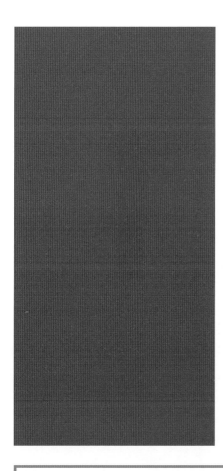

Presentation requirements:

A TOK presentation differs from a TOK essay in two key areas.

■ There is no prescribed title or question to use as a focus for investigation.

■ As a result, a student (or group) is required to create their own investigation focus.

To this end, students are required to do four things.

a. Find a real-life situation to use as a basis for exploration.

b. Generate an explicit knowledge question to focus the presentation on.

c. Develop this knowledge question by exploring the multiple associated issues or questions that arise from it (for example, the role of the ways of knowing, the differing positions presented by the areas of knowledge etc).

d. Explore the application/implications of the central knowledge question and any associated questions on other real-life situations.

The key focus of the TOK presentation is to show how TOK concepts (terms) and the knowledge questions that arise from them have a real-world application.

How your presentation is marked:

■ Out of 10 marks (worth 33% of the total mark for TOK)

■ By your teacher (a selection of Presentation Planning Documents are sent to the IB for external moderation)

■ Using achievement level descriptors, so not comparing your work to that of any other student but only against the descriptors (the official versions can be found on page 64 of the TOK guide)

■ With holistic or global judgment of the impression your presentation gives

■ If you present in a group, everyone in the group will be awarded the same mark

Developing a knowledge question for investigation

The structure and approach recommended in Section 3 (Applying TOK skills) should be followed when trying to generate knowledge questions from real-life situations.

Presentation structure

The TOK presentation diagram on the next page is an example of the overall structuring recommended by the IB for presentations.

The diagram is separated into two sections – the top is the 'real world' and the bottom is the 'TOK world'. It shows how a real-life situation can be developed to explore associated knowledge questions (thus moving from the 'real world' to the 'TOK world'). The implications and applications that arise from the investigation of knowledge questions need to be linked back to the real-life situation as well as to other examples where similar or contradictory themes can be observed (thus moving back out of the 'TOK world' to the 'real world').

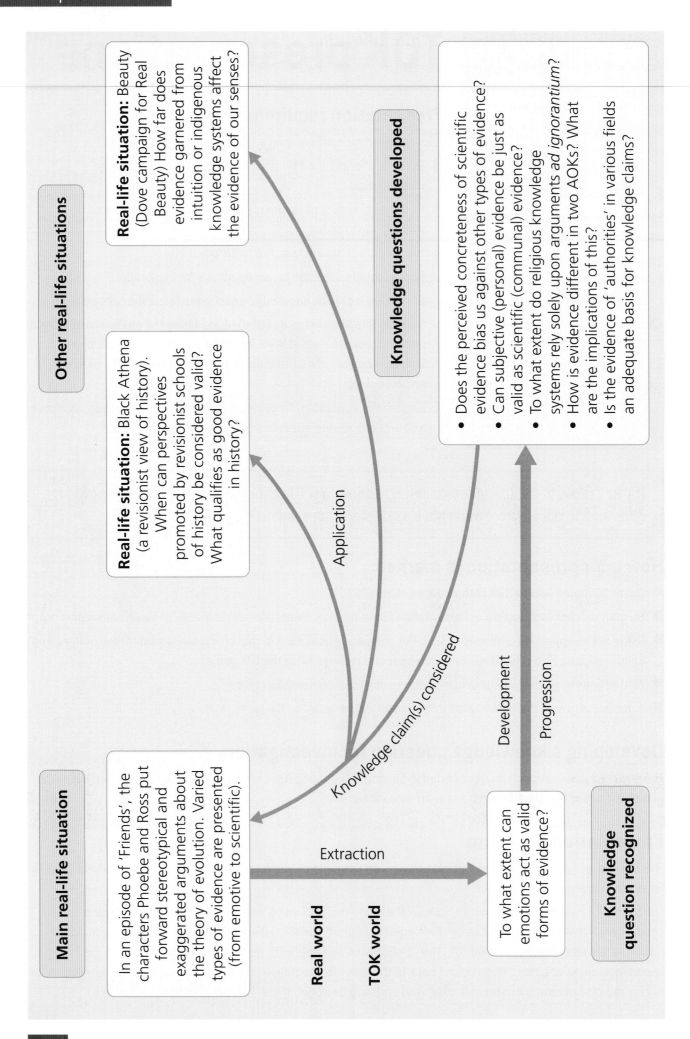

Other real-life situations

Real-life situation: Beauty (Dove campaign for Real Beauty) How far does evidence garnered from intuition or indigenous knowledge systems affect the evidence of our senses?

Real-life situation: Black Athena (a revisionist view of history). When can perspectives promoted by revisionist schools of history be considered valid? What qualifies as good evidence in history?

Knowledge questions developed

- Does the perceived concreteness of scientific evidence bias us against other types of evidence?
- Can subjective (personal) evidence be just as valid as scientific (communal) evidence?
- To what extent do religious knowledge systems rely solely upon arguments *ad ignorantium*?
- How is evidence different in two AOKs? What are the implications of this?
- Is the evidence of 'authorities' in various fields an adequate basis for knowledge claims?

Application

Knowledge claim(s) considered

Development

Progression

Main real-life situation

In an episode of 'Friends', the characters Phoebe and Ross put forward stereotypical and exaggerated arguments about the theory of evolution. Varied types of evidence are presented (from emotive to scientific).

Real world

TOK world

Extraction

To what extent can emotions act as valid forms of evidence?

Knowledge question recognized

Exploring the TOK presentation diagram

Stage 1: The presentation begins with the real-life situation under consideration. It is briefly introduced as a discussion between two characters from the series 'Friends' in which questions about the certainty of the theory of evolution are addressed.

Stage 2: In order to extract a knowledge question, some consideration for knowledge claims made in the RLS should be made. An example could be: 'Scientific evidence offers definitive proofs'.

Stage 3: A knowledge question can be built around the identification of one or more of the knowledge claims made in the real-life situation. Here the knowledge question is: 'To what extent can emotions act as valid forms of evidence?'

Stage 4: Associated knowledge questions can be developed in relation to the main one or two questions that result from that result from of a consideration of the knowledge claims identified in Stage 2.

Stage 5: TOK concepts (such as argument *ad ignorantiam*, personal evidence versus shared/communal evidence, authorities as evidence etc) are now linked back to the main real-life situation and also expanded upon to include other associated situations in which there is application. For example, the question relating to the value of subjective knowledge as a valid form of evidence could be applied to the field of history where questions of what constitutes 'good' evidence are always present.

▲ Phoebe and Ross argue about evolution

A NOTE ABOUT PRESENTATION GROUPS: Unlike the TOK essay which must be completed as an individual task, the TOK presentation can be done in pairs or groups of three (maximum permitted).

Keep in mind that in group presentations all candidates will receive the same grade as it is viewed as a collective effort and not as individual performances within a group dynamic.

Presentation notes

When preparing for the presentation, it is useful to prepare presentation notes. These notes should be written in the form of relevant paragraphs, with each paragraph covering a core or associated concept. As such they should adhere to the same structure as advised for TOK essays above:

Thesis → Development → Evidence → Balance → Analysis

Bear in mind that you must *not* read through these notes in your actual presentation. The purpose of writing them is to help you organize your thoughts and ensure a structured approach to the presentation. They are also useful for practising your presentation before actually doing it.

Ways of presenting

The significant difference, of course, between the TOK essay and the TOK presentation is that the latter does not need to be a written task (although the writing of presentation notes is useful for giving your presentation structure) and as such can take on a variety of forms.

In the example given here, the presentation could take the form of one of the following.

- A dialogue

For example, **a talk show** in which Phoebe and Ross (the characters from the sitcom 'Friends') are interviewed. The interview must touch upon some key knowledge questions that arise from this real-life situation and explore them through the responses the two characters provide. A scientist and perhaps a priest could also be brought into the conversation so as to develop reason as a way of knowing in relation to this question and also introduce the implications for religious knowledge systems.

- A dramatic skit

For example, **a role play** in which the debate between Phoebe and Ross could be developed further by introducing additional characters such as a scientist friend of Ross' and one of Phoebe's friends who is in advertising. The conversation between them could be developed as a casual discussion at a party but with some decisive and deliberate questions and comments to highlight the main knowledge questions.

- An audio-visual presentation using resources such as Prezi or Powerpoint

For example, **a conventional animated/slideshow** presentation that explores the different knowledge questions with varied relevant real-life examples in a visual manner.

The presentation planning document (Form TK/PPD)

As part of the new procedures governing the TOK presentation for examinations from 2015, the IB requests that all DP students submit a form in which five key questions need to be answered. A sample of these forms for each school will be used to moderate the presentation grades awarded by the school.

Below is an example of how these questions may be answered using the presentation exemplar above.

QUESTIONS:

1. Describe your real-life situation.

> I was watching an episode of the popular American sitcom 'Friends'. In this particular episode Phoebe and Ross have a debate about the theory of evolution because Ross, who is a palaeontologist, firmly believes in the theory of evolution and is quite shocked that Phoebe even questions the truth in that theory and rejects it on what he considers to be flimsy grounds (emotion, argument ad igorantiam etc).

2. State your central knowledge question.

The central knowledge question that I will address that arises out of this real-life situation is: To what extent can emotions act as valid forms of evidence.

3. Explain the connection between your real-life situation and your knowledge question.

In my real-life situation, one of the characters rejects a scientific theory that is one of the most significant scientific theories in the history of science based on a emotional response motivated by her religious beliefs and experiences. This response to the theory of evolution invited an inquiry into the types of evidence we would deem acceptable and what constitutes good evidence. It also invited an investigation into how different AOKs treat evidence.

4. Outline how you intend to develop your presentation, with respect to perspectives, subsidiary knowledge questions and arguments.

The presentation will explore issues relating to argument ad ignorantiam, authority and subjective (personal) evidence vs communal (shared) evidence in relation to the arts and natural sciences. It will focus on how evidence in one specific AOK may differ from others and that depending upon the discipline in question, different forms of evidence could be seen as equally viable, though perhaps not interchangeable. For instance, my personal evidence (the evidence of my senses) in relation to a work of art may be valid in the arts but not so valid when applied to the natural sciences where more consistently reproducible evidence is required....an exploration of the inherent bias afforded to scientific knowledge will also be addressed by looking at what factors make it so (e.g. authority, real-life application etc).

5. Show how your conclusions have significance for your real-life situation and beyond.

It becomes apparent that the nature of evidence has a direct bearing on how we know things in the different AOKs. Where in certain fields a specific type of evidence is valid, in others it is not. How each area defines what is sufficient or 'good' evidence is paramount for understanding how knowledge claims are made in each field. The role played by intuition (as a way of knowing) or cultural traditions (indigenous knowledge systems) may also shape the evidence of our senses by distorting, warping, magnifying or focusing the final mental image we have of any given situation. This, in turn, leads to either greater or lesser certainty with regards to claims made.

Presentation checklist

Applying all the skills involved in the Think TOK process should give you an excellent starting point for a high-scoring presentation. The aim of the presentation is to demonstrate that you know how the concepts which are central to TOK (knowledge questions, AOKs, WOKs, shared and personal knowledge) apply in the real world. Whether you're working individually or in a group, work through this checklist to check that your presentation meets the assessment requirements.

The basics:

✔ You can present individually, or in a group of two or three

✔ If you present alone, your presentation must be approximately 10 minutes long. If you present in a pair, it should be 20 minutes, and 30 minutes for a group of three

✔ Make sure that your presentation has a clear structure

✔ There are no rules about the format of your presentation, so you can be as creative as you like. However, remember that it is the content of your presentation which really matters, so don't get too distracted by fun presentation styles – choose a style that is appropriate for the real life situation you have chosen

✔ Practice your presentation in advance and prepare notes to help you present with confidence

✔ You will be required to submit a completed Presentation Planning Document (TK/PPD) before you give the presentation (see pages 92-93)

✔ Your school may allow you to attempt more than one presentation and select the best one for official marking. However, you cannot present on the same subject matter more than once

Check that you have:

✔ Clearly identified the real-life situation which is the starting point for your presentation

✔ Extracted and explained one well-defined knowledge question from the situation. Have you made it clear how the question arose from the situation?

✔ Shown your understanding of the knowledge question in relation to the perspectives of different people and cultures, from different AOKs and WOKs. Have you included evidence which both supports and counters the question?

✔ Discussed the ideas and arguments you've uncovered through this exploration in relation to the original situation

✔ Explained how the knowledge question and the insights you've uncovered through your analysis relate to other real-life situations

✔ Used real-life situations that are drawn from both your own personal experience and from the shared experiences of others

✔ Recognised your own personal perspective, with reference to alternative perspectives

Check that you have not:

✔ Spent too long describing situations or narrating events. Like the essay, the focus of the presentation is analysis. If you have to spend a long time describing real-life situations, they're probably not the right ones to use

✔ Concentrated on a subject-specific question. The question arising from your chosen situation must be a true knowledge question

✔ Made up your real-life situations, or used very common examples

✔ Made general statements such as 'Everyone knows…', 'We all believe that…'

✔ Used other people's ideas without crediting them

✔ Read your presentation from a script or pre-written essay

SECTION 5
Big ideas

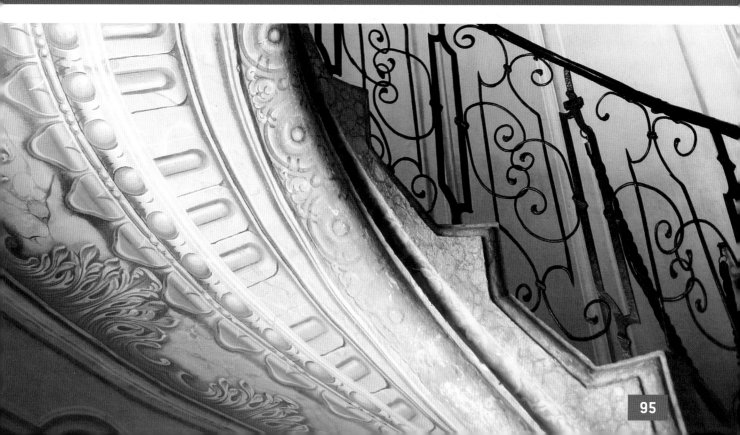

How to use this section

In this section, we have selected some of the most significant ideas human beings have had over the last few thousand years. Our choices are highly selective and we cannot possibly cover every idea in this small book, but it is a sample of how the idea of one person or one group of people has changed perceptions or had a huge impact on what came afterwards. To find out about more big ideas, we'd recommend the book *Ideas that Changed the World*, by Felipe Fernandez Armesto (2003).

As we said at the start of the book, TOK is not a philosophy course. But humans do not live alone in the world and our personal experience and contribution to the world relies on what we have learned from others.

The aim of this section is to give you a taste of how human imagination has changed our world — how ideas became actions and changed the path of history. What has this got to do with TOK, you may ask? Everything. It is our ability to generate ideas that has changed the human species from hunter-gatherer cave dwellers to complex civilizations over a relatively short space of time. The ability to ask questions and seek the answers at a high level is unique to the human species. We share our knowledge so that we can 'stand on the shoulders of giants'. That is what TOK is about.

If you want to know more about the ideas here, suggestions for further reading and research are given. The ideas are cross-referenced to the 'Big questions' in the rest of the book and can be used as springboards to get you started in analysing knowledge questions. Where words are given in **bold**, these are to give you a starting point for further reading on that topic.

There are tasks scattered among the big ideas in this section. You may want to develop some of these further and consider taking some of the ideas into your essay or presentation. We have also included lots of 'Think TOK' questions in this section (marked with a blue question mark in the margin) which you can use as starting points for class discussion, written tasks or your own thinking.

Remember the framework seen in Sections 2 and 3 so you can see the continuity in this section:

> 'Standing on the shoulders of giants' is a Western metaphor found in the writing of the Bernard of Chartres and Isaac Newton. It means to develop knowledge and understanding by building on the shared knowledge of those who came before.

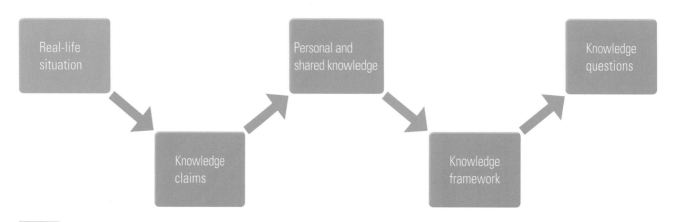

Big ideas

The ideas we discuss in the section are:

Ideas for communication

The idea of symbols and language

The idea of writing

Ideas about how we see the world

The idea that our senses are unreliable

The idea of a material world

The idea of rationalism

The idea of the scientific method

The idea of a spirit world

The idea of a creator

The idea of foretelling the future

Ideas about progress

The idea of time

The idea of a dynamic universe

The idea of a finite Earth

The idea of intelligent machines

Ideas about humans

The idea of the human mind and personal identity

The idea of art and the idea of beauty

The idea of universal morality

The idea of a superior human race or superior nation

The idea of human rights

Ideas about society

The idea of rules and laws

The idea of the state

The idea of the social contract

The idea of democracy

The idea of a just war

Big questions that are addressed in this section include:

- Can we know the nature of reality?
- Can we be certain of anything?
- How should we decide how to behave towards each other?
- How do we know if we are free to choose?
- How should we organize society?
- How do we know good government?
- How is scientific knowledge different from other types of knowledge?
- What is the relationship between language and truth?

TASK

Which of these are good **knowledge questions**?

A note on date notations

BCE = before Common Era, before the birth of Jesus Christ

BC = before Christ

CE = Common Era

AD = Anno Domini

Because the Christian calendar is used most frequently worldwide, the date of the birth of Christ is taken as the start of Common Era in the secular calendar.

TASK

You will see knowledge claims (in purple) and knowledge questions (in green) among the big ideas.

Think of other knowledge claims and questions as you read.

Ideas for communication

The idea of symbols and language

Humans first used symbols at least 30,000 years ago. Cavemen and women did not leave much behind, but they did leave their art, in the form of cave paintings and large standing stones, and their weapons such as flint arrowheads and stone axes. **Paeleolithic art** displays symbols in the form of gestures shown by the human forms painted on cave walls. There is evidence that they also produced a numbering system of dots and notches.

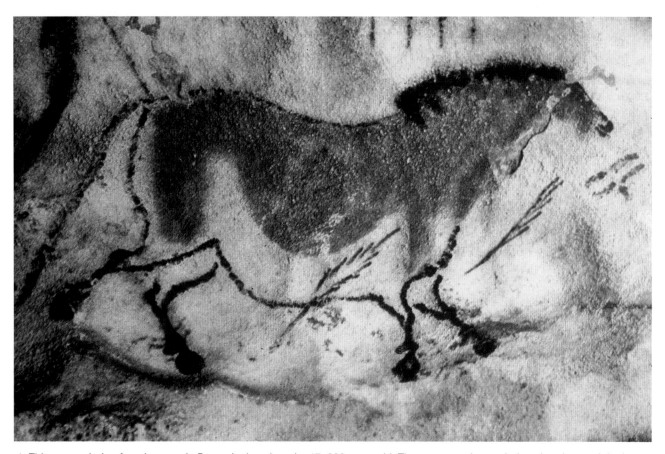

▲ This cave painting from Lascaux in France is thought to be 17, 300 years old. There seem to be symbols painted around the horse.

How language developed is not clear but social animals – from bees and ants to apes and whales – communicate with each other by signs, actions or sounds. Symbolic art is another way to communicate. Language is a system of symbols that we use to represent the world, to capture it, and to communicate what we think about it to others.

Is language an idea that humans invented or do we have a language instinct?

> *Symbols are the products of a collective human subconscious.*
>
> Carl Jung (1875–1961), *Man and His Symbols*, 1964

> *Language is not a cultural artefact that we learn the way we learn to tell time or how the federal government works. Instead, it is a distinct piece of the biological makeup of our brains. Language is a complex, specialised skill, which develops in the child spontaneously, without conscious effort or formal instruction …*
>
> Steven Pinker (1954–), *The Language Instinct*, 1994

> *There seems to be no substance to the view that human language is simply a more complex instance of something to be found elsewhere in the animal world. This poses a problem for the biologist, since, if true, it is an example of true 'emergence' — the appearance of a qualitative different phenomenon at a specific stage of complexity of organization.*
>
> Noam Chomsky (1928–), *Language and Mind*, 2006 (3rd edition)

 Do we learn languages quickly because their structure is already built into our brains? And, if grammatical structures are inherently the same, what does that do to the **Sapir-Whorf hypothesis**?

To what extent may knowing different languages change our concept of ourselves and the world?

That we communicate through language seems obvious, but Ludwig Wittgenstein (1889–1951), questioned the relationship between how we use language and what it really means. He thought that many misunderstandings came from our confused use of words and he encouraged us to *see* rather than to *interpret*.

📖 Find out more

For more on the Sapir-Whorf hypothesis, see Daniel Chandler's article on the topic (http://www.aber.ac.uk/media/Documents/short/whorf.html).

For more on **linguistic relativity hypothesis**, try Chris Swoyer's article 'Relativism' in *The Stanford Encyclopedia of Philosophy (Winter 2010 Edition)* (http://plato.stanford.edu/archives/win2010/entries/relativism/).

▲ My duck is your rabbit? What do you see? Wittgenstein asked his readers the same thing.

The idea of writing

How reliable is memory in sharing knowledge and discovered facts over time?

The first writing (5000–1500 BC) was possibly developed by the Sumerians, in modern-day Iraq. They used cuneiform script on clay tablets to keep accounts of sales, religious beliefs, and royal decrees.

Gilgamesh was a king of Sumeria who was written about on clay tablets found at Nineveh, Mesopotamia. In the Epic of Gilgamesh, he was said to be two-thirds god and one-third man, and to have ruled Uruk for 126 years. However, we have no physical evidence of his life and only know about him as he was written about.

Writing things down instead of relying on the oral tradition and memory made sharing knowledge easier and more reliable.

The beginning of written language marked the end of prehistory (which was not recorded) and start of recorded history – when we began to write, civilization started in earnest

▲ A carving depicting Gilgamesh, king of Sumeria

Writing was often (and still is) a way of keeping records of debts, invoices, and stock. It records personal histories, literature, and information. Language and writing are constantly developing. Nowadays, we use electronic records as much as paper ones now but still write. Voice recognition software may make learning to write redundant in future.

 Do you think learning to read could become unnecessary in time?

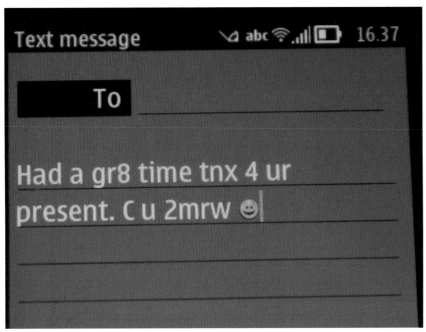

▲ A mobile phone text. Can you read it? Could your grandparents read it?

▲ Cunieform writing on a clay tablet

Ideas about how we see the world

The idea that our senses are unreliable

Our senses are not very good. Most animals have a sense of smell better than ours, we can't see as well as birds of prey, our hearing is poor, we only sense a small part of the electromagnetic spectrum, and we can't see ultra-violet light. Our night vision is terrible and we don't have sonar like bats.

Empiricism is a theory which claims that knowledge comes from sensory experience. To know something, you need to experience it and knowledge of something has to be based on evidence.

Dreams gave early humans an idea of other realities. They may have tried to recreate their dreams by using hallucinogenic plants, such as magic mushrooms. If our ancestors dreamed, or had hallucinations, of a successful hunt, for instance, this would produce a good feeling – especially if a real hunt was also successful. Representing the success of the hunt in an image on a cave wall could be an attempt to recall it or to influence the next hunt into being a good one. But we know that our senses are unreliable.

If you depend on senses alone for your view of reality, how can you be sure of your view of the world?

> In late 5th century BC, the philosopher Democritus said 'truth lies in the depths'. He meant that things are not always as they seem as our senses can mislead us.

> Traditionally, Maoris believe that the universe is a mirror reflecting the real world of the gods.

Distrusting our senses can take us to many other places. Illusions, visions, and imaginings cannot be tested through our senses as they are internal to the individual. Could they lead to faith and ideas of religion or magic? Abstract ideas such as infinity or eternity can be turned into a reality through art.

> Can we ever know the real world if we only have our senses to guide us?

> To what extent do our senses provide us with knowledge of the world as it really is?

Find out more

Claude Levi-Strauss (1908– 2009), The Savage Mind, 1962

▲ An example of Trompe l'oeil (visual illusion) in art where a 2-D image is made to look like a 3-D object

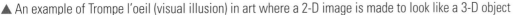

Optical illusions, like the one on the previous page, blur the boundaries between what is real and what is not. Knowing that some things we see are **illusions** could lead us to believe that everything is an illusion.

The Vedic text, Rigveda, and the Hindu Upanishads show that many have considered the illusory nature of our world. In the Hindu religion, the world is a dream of Brahman, the cosmic spirit, and so our human senses can tell us nothing. Māyā is a Sanskrit word which can be translated as 'illusion' and refers to the belief that we do not experience the world itself (because it is an illusion) but only experience a projection of it which we create ourselves. Our goal is to understand this and to recognize that there is no distinction between the individual and the universe.

Whether such a belief stops us from being an active participant in the world depends on who we are. It leads to **asceticism** and **mysticism** in some and to science and **secularism** in others.

Manoscritto miniato del « Rigveda ». Delhi, Forte rosso.

▲ Part of the Rigveda manuscript from the early 19th century.

 ## Find out more

To learn more about Hinduism, try Juan Mascaro's 1965 translation of the Upanishads.

How might emotion affect sense perception?

Here are 5 knowledge claims from different sources, all related to this knowledge question:

> 1. *People with synesthesia have heightened creativity.*
>   Jamie Ward et al, researchers at the University of Sussex, UK

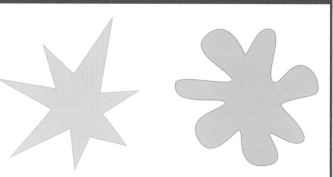

Synesthesia is a neurological condition in which senses get mingled together.

People with synesthesia may have any mixing of senses. They might experience a Mozart concerto as colours, hear a particular word and taste chocolate, taste an apple and see purple, know that the number eight is red, or that the letter C is yellow.

Up to 50 per cent of us have synesthesia – some common metaphors such as 'bitter wind' or 'loud dress', suggest that most people, to some extent, mix up their senses. Some painters, including Hockney and Kadinsky, have seen music as shapes and colours. The writers Vladimir Nabokov and Pat Duffy both say they have synesthesia.

 Look at the shapes at the top of this box. Which shape is Booboo? Which is Kiki?

2. *You are more likely to reach your goals if you are an optimist.*
   Suzanne Segerstrom in an article on the effects of multiple sclerosis (http://www.mstrust.org.uk/information/publications/fatigue/mood.jsp)

Optimists see the world as a glass half full, pessimists see it as half empty. The situation may be the same but your emotional state of mind determines how you will react. People who worry or are unhappy can be shown to have different psychological or physiological responses to those who are content.

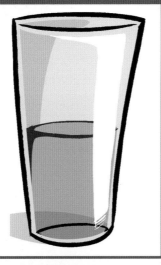

3. *Marital aggrandisement keeps marriages afloat.*
   Norm O'Rourke and Phillipe Cappeliez, researchers at the University of Ottawa

Norm O'Rouke and Phillipe Cappeliez, carried out research on 400 couples and found that many successful marriages rely on 'marital aggrandisement'. Each partner has an idealized view of a spouse which ignores negative beliefs and perceptions. These blind spots mean that they stay in a marriage for longer than if they were brutally honest about each others' faults. So slightly deluded thinking is better for marriages than cold reality.

4. *People with anorexia have a distorted self-image.*
   Jean Costa-Font and Mireia Jofre-Bonet, London School of Economics

A study carried out at the London School of Economics suggested that anorexia is a socially transmitted disease. People with anorexia, bulimia, and other food disorders have a distorted self-image and are preoccupied with their body image. Governments are justified in legally stopping magazines and fashion shows employing very skinny models as this reinforces the idea of an 'ideal', excessively thin body shape. Emotion allows sufferers to perceive themselves as someone who is too fat when they look in a mirror.

 Find out more

- Costa-Font J, Jofre-Bonet M (2012) 'Anorexia, body image and peer effects: evidence from a sample of European women', Economica (http://cep.lse.ac.uk/pubs/download/dp1098.pdf.)
- *Anorexia research finds government intervention justified*, Sarah Boseley, The Guardian, 01.03.12
- *Wasted: a Memoir of Anorexia and Bulimia*, Marya Hornbacher, 2006

5. Counterclaim to the KQ: It is sense perception that influences emotions.
   The Smell Report, Social Issues Research Centre, (http://www.sirc.org/publik/smell_emotion.html)

Our smell receptors are connected directly to the limbic system which is the part of the brain that deals with emotions. So we take in an odour and this changes our emotions even before we can name the smell.

We use scented candles to calm our moods, use perfumes to make ourselves attractive, and move away from bad smells.

TASK

In a group or in pairs, discuss the following real-world situations.

- Shops fill the air with scents to make us buy more – supermarkets with the smell of fresh citrus, clothes shops with expensive perfumes. How can this work?
- How we react depends on our emotional state. How might this affect soldiers in a war zone?
- We might assume that politicians make rational decisions based on fact. Do they or are their decisions influenced by how they feel at the time?

Find out more

More to look up on reliability of senses:

- The 1999 movie 'The Matrix', (and sequels) is an example of extreme scepticism – when we doubt accepted beliefs and need to test them.
- Do some research about Plato's analogy of the cave (375 BC).
- Watch this Youtube video about optical illusions: http://www.youtube.com/watch?v=4u64HDXoKVM.
- Explore Beau Lotto's 'lottolab' (http://www.lottolab.org/) and his TED talk (http://www.ted.com/talks/lang/en/beau_lotto_optical_illusions_show_how_we_see.html).
- *The Invisible Gorilla*, Christopher Chabris and Damiel Simons, 2010. You can watch a video of the selective attention test here: http://www.youtube.com/watch?v=vJG698U2Mvo.

The idea of a material world

That matter is all that there is and that everything is made up of atoms is an idea that humans have had for a long time. It is possible that early humans did not think about a spiritual world and simply lived for the moment and the next meal. We have no way of knowing exactly what they thought but we do have examples of their artwork that suggest that their imaginations ventured beyond the immediate, material world around them.

Sometime in the 6th century BC, Ajita Kesakambala, an Indian philosopher, proposed that the only world is the here and now. Everything is made up of earth, fire, water, and air and when a human dies, these elements that make him or her up are returned to the world. Offering alms or sacrifices is therefore pointless.

Democritus of Abders in 5th century BC agreed with this and said that everything is made of material particles, which are 'like specks of dust in a sunbeam'.

Epicurus (341–270 BC) went further and said that since the world is made of atoms which behave randomly, there can be no fate, no spirits, and so 'nothing to hope and nothing to fear'. He taught that we should only believe what we could see by direct observation and deduction, and that the way to fulfilment was to minimize harm to others and to oneself and to maximize happiness.

Materialists dismiss concepts such as 'mind', 'soul, 'spirit', and 'afterlife'. In parts of the Western world, materialism has become a new belief system. For some people in today's world, materialism is used to define a value system which values goods and belongings above intellectual or aesthetic activities. For example, going to visit an Apple store has been compared to entering a place of worship, where the goods have replaced the spirit world. For materialists, emotions are merely the result of chemical changes in our physical brains and bodies.

'Love is an intestinal irritation':
Denis Diderot (1713–84) was a French philosopher and writer who speculated on our free will and held a materialistic view.

Find out more

The Science Delusion, Rupert Sheldrake, 2012

The Axial Age 800–200 BC

Epicurus lived in what we call the Axial Age, meaning pivotal age, in which both the spiritual foundations and philosophical traditions of our world began. In this period also lived Moses (who laid the foundations of Judaism), Siddharta Gautama (Buddhism), Zoroaster (Zoroastrianism, which led to the development of monotheism), Confucius, Plato and the Greek sages. Other key figures of this age are Lao Tzu, Socrates, Parmenides, authors of the Upanishads and prophets of the Bible. Some say that the rest of civilization since that time has been a footnote to the thinkers of the Axial Age.

 Find out more

The Way to Wisdom: An Introduction to Philosophy, Karl Jaspers, 2003 (2nd edition)

The idea of rationalism

Rationalists believe that reason, as opposed to experience or emotion, gives us certainty of knowledge.

Renee Descartes is famous for his claim, 'Cogito ergo sum', commonly translated into English as 'I think therefore I am' (see 'Big questions' p144). He could not be sure of any evidence from his senses but only from the reasoning of his mind.

Rationalism (reasoning) and '**empiricism**' (experience) are two approaches that we use in understanding how we gain knowledge and much philosophy is focused on these.

The idea of the scientific method

What is it about the methodology of the natural sciences that makes the findings of natural sciences more reliable than those of some other AOKs?

Francis Bacon, an English polymath (an expert in many disciplines), is credited with developing the **inductive method** of science, whereby specific observations are turned into general laws. By making a general inference from many observations and then testing it, a scientific law or theory can be proposed and used to make predictions. So, it is through the experience of the senses (empiricism) and reason (rationalism) that science works.

Science is the means by which we try to understand the world around us through testable explanations. The scientific method (illustrated below) unpicks the processes involved in science and is often seen as a sequence of events: make observations – ask a question – do background research – construct a hypothesis – test the hypothesis – collect data – analyse data – check if it supports your hypothesis or not – share the results and conclusion – if enough experiments agree with yours, state a law. If enough laws can be explained with unified principles, it becomes a theory. To summarize:

observation → hypothesis → experiment (which is repeatable – by others, replicated and fair – with controls) → law → theory

It is this method that makes science 'science'. And it is this method that we are taught in science lessons at school. But science also involves imagination and intuition. Imagination in deciding what to observe, in making the hypotheses, in setting up the tests, in finding patterns and making conclusions. Intuition in making the leap to seeing the pattern or understanding the anomaly.

Also, there are problems with the inductive method of science – we are not as rational and logical as we would like to think. We may be observing the wrong

▲ Is this how you see a scientist?

things in the first place; because we expect to see something, we may think we see it; our technology may fool us; or by observing it, we may be changing the result. But the main concern with induction is that it goes from the specific to the general. Observing that the sun rises in the east every morning leads us to think that it always will – until it does not. If we see only white swans, we generalize that all swans are white – until we visit Australia, where swans are black.

The philosopher Karl Popper (1902–94) turned the idea of induction around by saying that scientists should test a hypothesis to try to prove it false, not to try to show it is true. That is because we cannot be sure that we have found every swan in the world to be able to say they are all white. It only takes one black swan to show the law 'all swans are white' is wrong. So Popper suggests we test to try to falsify hypotheses – **falsification** not verification. Theories can be provisionally accepted based on verification but are not absolutely proven even if all the evidence found so far supports the hypothesis – there is a chance that something will appear that does not support the hypothesis.

Deduction or deductive reasoning (from the general to the specific) can also be used in science – 'the sun always rises in the east so I predict it will rise in the east tomorrow'.

In his book *The Structure of Scientific Revolutions* (1962), Thomas Kuhn (1922–96) recognized step changes in how science explains the world and called these 'paradigm shifts'. In between these scientific revolutions, normal science goes on, until one or more scientists put forward a very different way of explaining the observations made. In Kuhn's thinking, Newton's laws of mechanics replaced Aristotle's ideas; Einstein's relativity replaced Newton's law; Wegener's theory of plate tectonics and continental drift replaced the idea of fixed continents. But Newton's laws are still valid on Earth if not in space, so, in fact, it is more a case of evolution than of revolution.

How these step changes occur is not only due to rational scientific thought. It is far more complex, and depends on human emotions (such as envy, ambition, greed), social change (for example, how the internet spreads ideas) and whether or not the time is right (Darwin's theory of evolution).

Science differs from **pseudoscience** in that its hypotheses can be tested.

 **Find out more**

Cargo Cult Science, Richard Feynman, 1974 (http://www.lhup. edu/~DSIMANEK/cargocul.htm)

The idea of a spirit world

Human imagination soon allowed us to believe that there are spirits in other living things and in inanimate objects. Once we began to think that some of our being was immaterial (call it a mind, soul, or character), it was a simple step to give other objects the same attribute, whether they were stones, the sun, or the sky. Similarly, physical events could be seen as supernatural phenomena.

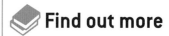

Find out more

Mortal Questions, Thomas Nagel, 1980

> *Everything is full of gods.*
> Thales of Miletus (585 BC)

Once we believed in a spirit world, we wanted to communicate with it. The ancient Greeks knew that their gods lived on Mount Olympus. Mayan kings induced visionary states through bloodletting and narcotics in the hope of seeing the ancestral spirit. The Melevi Order of Sufis (known as Whirling Dervishes) perform the Sama dance which represents a journey of man's spirit to the Perfect.

The existence of a spirit world allows us to think that we might become part of it after our physical death. The belief that death leads to an **afterlife** is first evidenced in **grave goods**, which are objects (or people) buried with the dead to go with them and be used in the next life. In traditional Chinese funerals, paper replicas of money, houses, and other items are burnt to ensure that the spirit has a comfortable afterlife.

We have found buried grave goods from as long ago as 40,000 years. Monuments to commemorate the dead can be huge, such as **the Great Pyramid of Cheops**.

How do we judge the evidence for an afterlife?

We constantly change as we age and as time passes, yet we are still the same person, even if all of our atoms have been replaced. To many people, this suggests that there is logic in the idea of life after physical death. Many civilizations believed that inherited wealth could transcend death and assumed that a rich man continues to be a rich man in the next life. On the other hand, others believe that souls are weighed at death to determine if a good life was lived; if a life was badly lived, there may be punishment in the afterlife.

▲ The Northern Lights - natural or supernatural?

▲ Terracotta army of Qin Shi Huang, the first emperor of China, Xian, China 3rd century BC

▲ Death mask of Pharaoh Tutankhamun, Egypt 1323 BC

In ancient Egypt, the god Anubis would weigh the soul of the dead against a feather. If you committed many wrongs, your soul would be heavy. The lighter your soul, the better the place you would go.

In the three religions of the Book (Judaism, Islam, and Christianity) as well as in Buddhism and Hinduism, there is a belief in **a judgment day**. In Buddhism, **reincarnation** depends on the merit gained in this life.

We erect gravestones, tombs, mausoleums, and monuments which continue to mark the identity of the dead for much longer than the lifetime of the individual.

▲ Anubis weighing a soul against a feather

➡ Why do we commemorate the dead with monuments and gravestones?

Ancestor worship and **veneration of the dead** is practised in many religions. The Catholic Church venerates saints who are created, or canonized, by the Pope as holy beings able to communicate between ordinary people and God. In the Chinese Taoist tradition, ancestors are venerated to ensure their well-being in the afterlife and may be called upon to provide help to the living.

There is a strong social and cultural need to remember ancestors in the family lineage and for filial piety throughout many world religions.

> 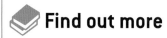 **Find out more**
>
> *The Divine Comedy*, Dante Alighieri, 1321

The idea of a creator

We are amazingly complex organisms and the world in which we live is ordered, beautiful, and seems to 'work'. Some believe this could not have been formed by natural processes alone. There must be an overarching purpose to the world (and our lives) and a creator who made the world and us.

➡ To many people, the human eye suggests a similar argument. How can such a complex organ have been formed through evolution by mutation and natural selection? A watch is made for a purpose – to tell the time – so there must be a watchmaker somewhere. The world is made for a purpose – so there must be a creator of the world. This argument was made by William Paley in his book *Natural Theology* (1802).

In his book *The Blind Watchmaker* (1986), Richard Dawkins proposed a counter-argument to Paley's idea. Dawkins believes that natural selection can produce complex structures without the need for an overarching purpose from God.

> **TASK**
>
> There are many arguments for and against the existence of God. Try these two websites for a start and then find other sources. Do you agree or disagree with the arguments for the existence of God?
>
> - http://theologicalstudies.org/resource-library/philosophy-dictionary/86-4-primary-arguments-for-gods-existence
> - http://theologicalscribbles.blogspot.co.uk/2009/05/great-arguments-against-gods-existence.html

The idea of foretelling the future

We appear to have some influence on our own future. Our actions have reactions and we are accountable for what we decide to do or not do. It is also the case that other people or forces can influence our future.

Astrology has had a place in foretelling the future since the time of Babylonian astrologers. That the position of the stars at the time of our birth can influence our fate and character could seem like a wild claim, yet many believe in it. Science has found little evidence to support the belief in astrology, other than the influence the stars and planets have on the magnetic fields on Earth, yet the grouping of stars into constellations has a long history.

In the ancient Greek and Roman worlds, **oracles** were people that could foretell the future because the gods spoke through them. In China, in the Shang dynasty (1600–1046 BC), oracle bones were used to foretell the future.

▲ The constellation of Ursa Major (the Great Bear) with the 'Plough' within it marked.

Séances, reading tea leaves, studying chicken entrails, crystal balls, the palms of our hands – all these are more are ways to 'see the future'. Another common belief is that we can change the future by sacrifice or prayer.

?➤ Do you try to change the future by an indirect action? For example, do you think that watching your team play sport on TV will influence the result?

Art and religion

Sacred art and the idea of icons that represent gods and other religious beings have a mixed history. Islam bans icons, meaning that non-representational art has a strong tradition in Islamic history. With the Old Testament as its basis, the Jewish faith bans idolatry:

You shall not make for yourself any idol, nor bow down to it or worship it.

You shall not misuse the name of the Lord your God.

These commandments are in the Old Testament of the Bible and yet Christianity, which also takes the Bible as its holy book, has used religious art for much of its existence.

Christianity has taken various stands on religious images. In Byzantium, **iconoclasm** (image-breaking) in 726–787 and 814–842 banned all religious images and many works of religious art were destroyed.

Medieval Christians used religious representational art to inspire worship among the many who could not read, seemingly ignoring the iconoclasm of the commandments.

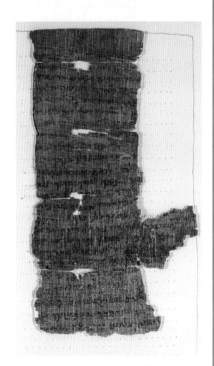
▲ The Nash Papyrus, a 2000 year old document of the Hebrew 10 commandments.

Why are religion and the arts intertwined in most cultures?

- The arts bring religion to life – they visualize it, tell a story, make music about it, dramatize it.
- If most of the population is illiterate, visual art or story-telling is a way to pass on the information and keep the community together.
- Religion is not temporal or material – to make it seen and heard, the arts are employed.
- The arts make religious characters more real by giving them faces and features. They provide something to venerate and meditate upon.
- The arts transcend generations and can pass on the value system and history of religion.

▲ Arabic calligraphy and patterns

▲ The Last Supper, by Leonardo da Vinci (1452–1519)

TASK

Choose a religion you are familiar with. Select an art form (it could be music, visual arts, dance, film, poetry, fiction, drama) in which it is portrayed.

Consider the relationship between the religion and the art form by answering this question: In what way is the religion depicted in the art?

Now consider these questions:

- How much of the depiction is based on the artist's perception and how much on the knowledge framework of the religion?
- What does the art add to your knowledge of the religion?
- How does the depiction influence your personal view of the religion?
- How is the community influenced by this depiction of the religion?
- What is the purpose of the depiction?

Ideas about progress

The idea of time

We have all grown up with the idea of time. Sometimes, we use digital clocks, and sometimes we use analogue ones with hands that go round and round on a face.

Do you think of time as linear or cyclical? How do you think animals recognize time? Does time go faster for you sometimes? Why?

Can how you tell the time alter your perception of it?

Time is change. We can see change all around us. Plants germinate, grow, set seed, and die. We are born as babies, grow up, age and eventually die. The sun passes overhead each day from sunrise to sunset. The moon waxes and wanes in cycles.

Early peoples measured time in cycles – the cycle of crop growth, the cycles of the moon and stars, the seasons. They may have used tally sticks and standing stones to mark the passage of the sun.

▲ Stonehenge, England was built 2000 BC. Here it is photographed at sunrise on the mid-summer equinox

The Antikythera Mechanism

The Antikythera Mechanism is a device with more than 30 gear wheels from the 1st century BC. Possibly designed by Archimedes in Sicily, it is an astronomical clock of amazing sophistication. We think that its purpose was to predict solar and lunar eclipses and to show the position of the planets of the solar system. It is the world's first analogue computer.

▲ The Antikythera Mechanism, on display at the National Archaeological Museum of Athens

Once humans started timekeeping, it was inevitable that we then anticipated events, organized memories, prioritized tasks, and worked together in collaborative ventures.

But is time linear or cyclical? Or is it both? Does it exist outside our minds?

We now accept natural cycles (the year, the month) and linear time as we grow older. Traditional societies such as the Nuer of Sudan marked the passing of time through events such as the growth of livestock and initiation ceremonies. Old Testament writers marked time by generations:

> Abraham begat Isaac; and Isaac begat Jacob; and Jacob begat Judas and his brethren; / And Judas begat Phares and Zara of Thamar; and Phares begat Esrom; and Esrom begat Aram;

Matthew, Chapter 1:2

The **Big Bang** theory of how the universe began 13.7 billion years ago supports the concept of linear time – but it also raises the question 'when does time stop?'

The story of Genesis in the Bible marks linear time in its telling of God creating the Earth in seven days. This idea was adopted in Islam and Christianity and so the modern world tends to think of linear time. The concept of linear time suggests that history is progressive and cannot be repeated. In Christianity, when Jesus Christ died for man's sins, time could not be cyclical as His Second Coming heralded the end of the world and Judgment Day.

 Find out more

- *Time's Arrow,* Steven J Gould, 1998, is a very readable study of time.
- *Time in History,* G J Witrow, 1989, looks at different cultures' perspectives on time.

Linear time is a central issue in Christian theology. If Christ's coming occured at a particular time and was to save humankind from eternal damnation, what happens to all those who lived before Christ came to Earth and to those who had never heard of him? If God is omniscient (all knowing) and so knows who will be saved and who will not, then we do not have **free will** to choose our path, as it is predetermined. This dilemma has created much debate over the centuries. Do we live a good life and do good deeds in the hope of earning salvation, or are we **predestined** to do what we do and faith alone connects us to God? That question and its interpretation has led to various Christian denominations being formed and unending controversy.

 Find out more

Search for 'The Antikythera Mechanism: World's oldest computer' on YouTube (http://www.youtube.com/watch?v=Ly3cpBFWF-o) to watch a 50-minute film on the Mechanism and its history.

The concept of *Badā* (revealing after concealing) in Shia Islam allows for God not to have fixed the course of human history, meaning that humans can change it – in this way there is no predestination in our fates.

In science, the idea of **relativity** undermined the idea that time is a constant. Einstein produced the theory of special relativity in 1905 and of general relativity in 1916. These changed our view of spacetime because, if the speed of light (300 million meters per second) is a constant, then time and distance must be relative to it – so time cannot be constant.

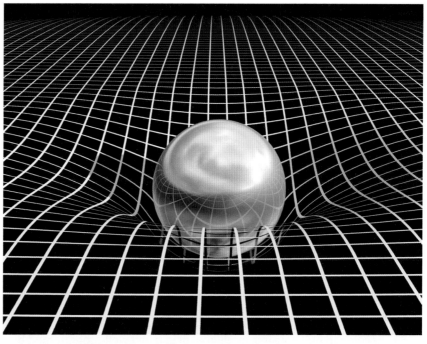

▲ Large bodies in space warp spacetime causing gravity

The idea of a dynamic universe

Many believe that the world was created by a supernatural being at one moment and has been unchanged or static since then. This is **creationism**. A belief in a moment of creation takes many forms in many religions. Some believe in the infallibility of holy books and so, for example, the story of God creating the world in Genesis is taken as literal by some believers.

Scientific evidence from fossils, geology, and the study of life on Earth indicates that the Earth is about 4.5 billion years old and has been changing since it was formed. Science has proven that species change through mutation and natural selection leading to **evolution**.

▲ Fossil turtle from 220 million year old rocks

That the Earth and the universe are dynamic (undergoing constant change) is widely accepted and that allows for change in the economic, political, and social senses. The idea of progress is fundamental to our economic model in which economic growth is the key to removing people from poverty and starvation.

> *You can never step twice into the same river.*
> Heraclitus, Greek philosopher (535–475 BC)

Time, change and progress, all lead to …

The idea of a finite Earth

Throughout most of our civilization, the idea that the Earth's resources were limited seemed impossible. Humans were fighting to live in a hostile environment and it appeared that there was no limit to the natural goods we exploited, be it fish, wood, or land.

It is only in the last 100 years that we have recognized that resources cannot meet our insatiable demand. The concept of **sustainability**, leaving enough for future generations to meet their needs, is relatively new in human history.

 Find out more

Collapse: How Societies Choose to Fail or Succeed, Jared Diamond, 2005

The idea of intelligent machines (or artificial intelligence – A.I.)

In 1950, a thought experiment was devised by Alan Turing, a mathematician and computer pioneer. The experiment – known as the Turing Test – was designed to test whether a machine could think. It is still used today.

In the test, a human has to pose questions to another being, but does not know if he is addressing another human or a machine. After some time, the person asking the questions has to decide if he is talking to a human or a machine.

 Is 'Siri' developed by Apple Inc. intelligent or is it just well-programmed by humans?

 Find out more

John Searle developed the Turing test in the 'Chinese Room Argument' (1980) (http://plato.stanford.edu/entries/chinese-room/).

TASK

Your aim is to create the tallest possible structure using whatever materials are easy to acquire – newspaper, tissue paper, waste packaging, sticky tape, cardboard tubes, card, paper clips etc. (Or the glider that can fly the furthest, a parachute for an egg so it will not break on landing – any task involving making something for your chosen challenge.)

Work in teams, agree on a time limit for completion, and have a prize ready for the winning team.

After the challenge, discuss these questions:

- How did you decide what to make?
- What knowledge did you use?
- Did this knowledge assist you in the design?
- How much imagination did you need?
- What were the challenges you faced?
- Why did your product work or not work? What could you have done differently?

Can we have knowledge without imagination?

We have knowledge when we apply data and information to answer 'how' questions. Imagination is when we create images or feelings within our minds. Sometimes imagination helps us in applying our knowledge.

Knowledge explains aspects of the world to us and allows us to understand, predict, and problem solve. It can be knowledge specific to an individual – personal knowledge – or knowledge gained by a group working together over time or space – shared knowledge. Imagination allows us to form mental images without using our sense perception and to think about the 'what ifs'.

Let's unpick some of the knowledge claims which could be used to explore this question:

1 *Imagination is more important than knowledge.*
Albert Einstein, German physicist, 1879–1955

In 1929, the journalist George Viereck asked Albert Einstein: 'How do you account for your discoveries? Through intuition or inspiration?' Einstein replied:

'Both. I sometimes *feel* I am right, but do not *know* it. When two expeditions of scientists went to test my theory I was convinced they would confirm my theory. I wasn't surprised when the results confirmed my intuition, but I would have been surprised had I been wrong. I'm enough of an artist to draw freely on my imagination, which I think is more important than knowledge. Knowledge is limited. Imagination encircles the world.'

 Find out more

- Find out more about Einstein's interview with Viereck: http://www.timeshighereducation.co.uk/story.asp?storycode=172613
- Brains on display! http://blogs.sundaymercury.net/weirdscience/2012/03/einsteins-brains-go-on-display.html

2 *If you're not prepared to be wrong, you'll never come up with anything original.*
Sir Ken Robinson, English author, speaker, and international advisor on education, Changing Paradigms
(http://www.thersa.org/events/video/archive/sir-ken-robinson)

- Our education system produces good factory workers, not creative thinkers.
- We become less creative with age – we get educated out of it.
- There is a hierarchy of subjects (maths/science at the top, arts, dance, woodwork near the bottom).
- Talents have to be nurtured, not abandoned.

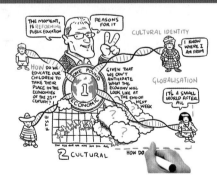

 Find out more

- A TEDtalk from Ken Robinson: http://www.ted.com/talks/ken_robinson_says_schools_kill_creativity.html
- The English philosopher Bertrand Russell (1872–1970) in his essay on 'Education and Disciplines' says that any education should consist of a 'conception of the ends of life and a science of psychological dynamics' in which children have a joy in learning, take responsibility, are friendly to new people and new ideas, and have some degree of freedom. But they have to be taught consideration for others by adults. (http://www.davemckay.co.uk/philosophy/russell/russell.php?name=education.and.discipline)

3 *Watson and Crick did not discover DNA but did produce an accurate model of its structure.*
Leslei A. Pray, 'Discovery of DNA Structure and Function, Watson and Crick', 2008 (http://www.nature.com/scitable/topicpage/discovery-of-dna-structure-and-function-watson-397)

It was only by relying on previous work by other scientists that Watson and Crick in 1953 proposed the correct structure of DNA. DNA was discovered by Miescher, a Swiss scientist in the late 1860s. Its chemical composition was worked out by Chargaff and Levene as well as others. Chargaff discovered that the amount of adenine and thymine in DNA is about equal as is the amount of cytosine and guanine (the base pairs). Rosalind Franklin and Maurice Wilkins showed that DNA was helical through x-ray diffraction and Linus Pauling developed 3D molecular models of it.

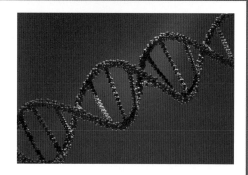

Only because of the accumulation of knowledge from these and others were Watson and Crick in a position to produce a double helix model with base pairing and a sugar-phosphate backbone. Scientific discovery may have some imagination in it but it is based on hard work, methodical analysis, and the testing of hypotheses.

4 *The noblest pleasure is the joy of understanding.*
Claude Monet, French painter, (1840–1926)

- Monet's paintings were the expression of the world he felt, not literal images.
- He wanted to show universal truths by capturing a moment, a fragment of time with its particular light effects.
- He painted outdoors and used small brush strokes, showing a different way of seeing.
- But he had great skill in painting techniques which he learned over years.

5 *Beauty is truth and truth beauty, that is all Ye know on earth, and all ye need to know.*
From 'Ode on a Grecian Urn', John Keats, 1819

- Keats was an English Romantic poet (1795–1821); he died aged 25 of tuberculosis.
- Romanticism is the belief that the perception of reality is only understood through imagination. Unlike Realism or Classicism which generalize from experience, Romanticism tells of the world as it should be, not as it is. It is the triumph of emotion over reason and the sensory experience over the intellect. It is personal knowledge of imagination through which the world is understood – we should think of holding a lamp to the world and seeing it better, rather than holding a mirror to the world and seeing it reflected.

 Find out more

- Keats' Kingdom: http://www.keatsian.co.uk/
- Find out more about Romanticim here: http://www.textetc.com/traditional/romanticism.html

Ideas about humans

The idea of the human mind and personal identity

Is the mind separate from the body or is it merely the activity of our brain cells. Do we have a soul?

We are conscious of our consciousness, at least when we are awake. We know who we are and can think regardless of whether our body is inactive or active. So it is not surprising that we developed the idea of a mind separate from the body. The philosopher Gilbert Ryle called this 'the ghost in the machine'; others call it **dualism**. Descartes saw mind and body as completely separate. If you believe in dualism, a supernatural world, in which the mind (or soul) can exist after death of the physical body, becomes possible. So does reincarnation, where the same soul exists in a new body.

But our body is always renewing itself when we are alive. We are made up of different atoms now to when we were born but are still the same person. At least we think we are. Why might you think you are the same person you were when you were born?

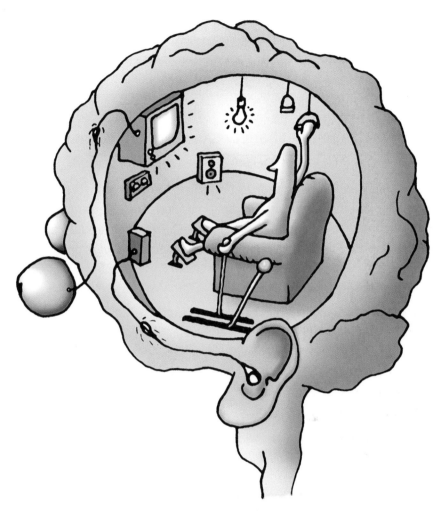
▲ The ghost in the machine

The Theseus paradox

If all the parts of a ship are replaced over time, is it still the same ship?

This paradox was quoted by Plutarch, a philosopher in ancient Greece. It was later added to by Thomas Hobbes (1588–1679) who asked, if all the parts of the original ship were collected and reassembled, is this the same ship? Are either the original ship?

What if someone else's brain was transplanted into your head. Who would you be? The body person or the brain person? Most of us would say the brain person because we feel that our brain holds the key to who we are, our memories, and character. So would your brain kept alive in a laboratory flask still be you (see also 'Big questions' p120)?

"There is not any other Substance than *Spirit*, or that which perceives."

If we know about the world only because we are able to perceive it using our senses, then what happens to the world when we *stop* perceiving it?

This question, which at first sight might seem to be rather strange, or perhaps even silly, had, for George Berkeley, only one answer. Berkeley argued that objects can only exist when they are being perceived, since the idea of an 'unperceived' object is logically impossible: we can't conceive of something existing that we are unable to perceive; therefore, objects only exist if and when we are able to perceive them.

Like Descartes, Berkeley said that we know *we* exist, but beyond that, only our ideas of the external world were real.

Berkeley's idea might be the only one in philosophy that's ever been summed up in limerick form. It was written from the perspective of a Berkeley-believing student looking at a tree in a courtyard (quad) at university.

Hang on one moment! This is truly weird!

The idea that the world somehow springs into being when we are looking at it, and then disappears when we're not, has struck many people as truly bizarre. But Berkeley had an answer to this criticism. As a Christian, Berkeley believed that God – who is, in the Christian tradition, in all places at once, and sees everything – ensured that the world did *not* just appear and disappear at random. For Berkeley, God saw everything at all times, protecting the world from the sort of random behaviour pointed out by his critics.

I

There was a young man who said, 'God
Must think it exceedingly odd
    If he thinks that this tree
    Continues to be
When there's no one about in this Quad.'

II

Dear Sir:
    Your astonishment's odd:
I am always about in the Quad
    And that's why the tree
    Will continue to be,
Since observed by
    Yours faithfully,
                        GOD.
                Ronald Knox

"I refute it *thus*."

'After we came out of the church, we stood talking for some time together of Bishop Berkeley's ingenious sophistry to prove the nonexistence of matter, and that every thing in the universe is merely ideal. I observed, that though we are satisfied his doctrine is not true, it is impossible to refute it. I never shall forget the alacrity with which Johnson answered, striking his foot with mighty force against a large stone, till he rebounded from it—'I refute it thus'

From James Boswell's, *Life of Samuel Johnson*

Although Berkeley's ideas have struck many people as unbelievable, it's proved very difficult to show convincingly why Berkeley is actually wrong. Samuel Johnson, above, and his friend James Boswell were just some of the first people to find Berkeley's ideas unacceptable, yet very hard to disprove. Johnson's attempt to show Berkeley's error by banging his foot against a rock – and getting a sore foot in return – hasn't struck many philosophers since as particularly convincing.

Lord Byron's 1824 poem 'Don Juan' expressed an uneasiness with Berkeley's views similar to that of Johnson and Boswell.

When Bishop Berkeley said 'there was no matter,'
    And proved it—[I]t was no matter what he said:
    They say his system 't is in vain to batter,
    Too subtle for the airiest human head;
And yet who can believe it?

The great twentieth-century philosopher Bertrand Russell thought he had proved Berkeley wrong once and for all. Russell said that we know some statements to be true without experiencing them. For example, 'the number of possible multiplications of two integers is infinite', a mathematical statement that is undoubtedly true, but unable to be 'perceived' by the senses. If you believed Berkeley, Russell argued, then you'd have to deny that mathematical theorems are true. But, Russell continued, theorems are true *by definition*. Therefore, Berkeley was wrong.

Is there nothing?

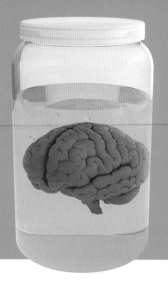

A story about brains in jars
Imagine that one day you meet a mad scientist.

He takes you to his laboratory, where he shows you an odd sight: in a jar on the table, there is a human brain, called Mary. The brain is connected by a bundle of wires to a very large computer. The mad scientist tells you that this brain (Mary) is being kept alive, and that the computer is sending signals down the wires that stimulate Mary to believe certain things. Mary, the scientist tells you, thinks that she is alive, and is living a pretty normal life. But this is an illusion. When Mary thinks that she is waking up in the morning and drawing the curtains to her bedroom, what is actually happening is that the scientist's computer is sending signals to Mary to make her *believe* that this is what she is doing. In the same way, when Mary thinks she's getting on the bus to go to the shops, this is just the computer tricking her into thinking she's doing this. In reality, Mary is – as you can see – just a brain in a jar on a table.

In some ways, this is just a story. Computers don't yet exist that can stimulate a brain to feel such complex feelings. But the point of the story is different, and the key question is this: **can you *prove* that *you* are not Mary, the brain in a jar?**

The 'brain in a jar' problem is one of the oldest in philosophy. Hundreds of years before computers were invented, Descartes put forward a similar idea with his thought-experiment that an 'evil demon' could be controlling all your thoughts. And almost two thousand years before Descartes, the ancient Greek philosopher Plato put forward a similar (although not quite the same) idea with his 'analogy of the cave'. With this long history, it's not surprising that the big question posed by the 'brain in a jar' – how do you know that *you* are not in a jar? – has proved extremely tough to answer.

Is this an answer?

Hilary Putnam (1926), the American philosopher who first wrote out the 'brain in a jar' question, also thought he had a solid answer to it. According to Putnam's rather complex argument, it would be *logically impossible* of us to think of ourselves as brains in jars if we actually *were* brains in jars. If this sounds ridiculous, then don't worry: Putnam knew his argument sounded odd. It works like this. A brain in a jar could have no *real* knowledge of the outside world, because it had never truly experienced it. A brain in a jar could never, for example, really know what a tree was, because it had never in reality seen one. Although the brain might *think* it had seen a tree, this would be (we know) just an illusion put into its mind by the computer. In the same way, the jar-brain could never have a true understanding of what a brain in a jar would look like, because it had never experienced a real jar, or scientist, or computer. So a brain in a jar could never truly imagine itself as a brain in a jar.

Philosophy *vs.* Science

Hilary Putnam may have proved it 'logically impossible' for the 'brain in a jar' idea to be true. But is his argument *really* convincing? Some scientists would probably say 'no'...

Plugging in your brain to a small electric current can dramatically affect how you feel.

Relatively frequently, people with Parkinson's disease (which, among other things, can lead you to make uncontrolled movements), have electrodes inserted into their brains. When a current is passed through these, the uncontrolled movement often stops. However, some people who have been treated with this 'deep-brain stimulation' have developed remarkable side effects. One patient, when the current was switched on, began to find the whole world exceptionally funny. He simply could not stop laughing – not because he physically could not shut his mouth, but because he genuinely began to find his surroundings hilarious. He even made the doctors treating him crack up. One of the doctors, the patient pointed out, had a very long nose like the film character Cyrano de Bergerac. *Everyone* (even the long-nosed doctor) also found this funny, and they couldn't stop laughing either.

After a while, however, all this laughter became tiring for the patient, and he asked the doctors if they could return him to his previous mental state. The doctors had no problem doing this: they simply switched off the current going into his brain.

So, a scientist might say: If your brain is plugged into the right equipment, there is solid evidence that scientists can change how you feel and how you behave. It's impossible to deny this – there have been examples of people who have been made to feel severely depressed, or even just moderately amused after the same treatment – meaning that we also can't deny that future progress might lead to scientists being able to control patients' brains in all sorts of other ways, too. So, the 'brain in a jar' idea has to be possible.

Deep-brain stimulation: evidence that you *could* be a brain in a jar?

What would a philosopher (like Putnam) say in response to this? Has science defeated philosophy? Would Putnam admit he got it wrong? Or would he come up with a counter-argument?

"Rather than continuing to seek the truth, simply let go of your views."

Gautama Buddha (c.483–c.411 BC)

You don't exist

Three fundamental Buddhist beliefs provide clear answers to some major life questions. Here's a summary.

One: All life is suffering (*Dukkha*)

Buddhists are not miserable – many (such as the current Dalai Lama) are known for their sense of humour. But all Buddhists believe strongly that all earthly life is characterized by pain and suffering. That's because even things we think are unquestionably good will at some point come to an end, causing us pain. In the end, Buddhists point out, each of us, and all of our loved ones, will die. And that's why all life is suffering.

Two: Everything is impermanent (*Anicca*)

This follows on from the realization that all life is suffering. The suffering in life comes from the fact that nothing lasts. Even the biggest mountains will wear down in time, Buddhists point out, and all our happy feelings will one day come to an end.

Three: 'You' don't exist (*Anatta*)

This is the trickiest, but perhaps also the most important, concept to grasp. Because Buddhists see everything as impermanent, it follows that the concept of 'I' cannot exist. We can't think of 'ourselves' as unchanging or in any sense permanent. 'We' are just made up of ever-changing sensations and an ever-changing physical form. Just like everything else, 'we' don't exist. We are just a fleeting collection of phenomena and cells.

Neither does anything else

The world is empty: *Śūnyatā*

The world is impermanent and you don't exist. This is the starting point for all Buddhist belief. This, for many Buddhists, has one big implication: nothing else truly exists either — the world is, in other words, 'empty' of all real things (Śūnyatā). Understanding this is, many Buddhists argue, very hard: they *don't* argue that there is absolutely nothing at all 'out there' in the world. But they *do* argue that the true nature of reality is only visible to a very few enlightened people. This small bunch of believers can, in turn, see the true 'emptiness' of what the rest of us see and feel. What makes the enlightened special is that they have 'let go' (as the Buddha said) of the false view of reality that most of us have. The Śūnyatā doctrine wasn't put forward by the Buddha himself, but was developed later in the Mahāyāna tradition, and particularly in the *Prajñāpāramitā* ('Perfection of Wisdom') literature.

> **Reason well from the beginning and then there will never be any need to look back with confusion and doubt.**
>
> The Fourteenth Dalai Lama (1935–)

The idea of art and the idea of beauty

The prehistoric and ancient worlds often made use of representational art. Art could tell a story, educate, persuade, and be aesthetically or emotionally pleasing. Plays, sculpture, mosaics, and music all performed these roles.

Art was associated with beauty – whatever that is.

In visual arts, whether beauty can exist without an observer depends on whether you are a realist or anti-realist. An anti-realist would believe that aesthetic judgment is tied to the observer. Is 'Beauty in the eye of the beholder' or does it emerge from a set of absolute rules based on the natural world?

When we divorced art from representation and it became abstract and expressionist, appreciation became more about understanding the emotions and message of the artist or the observer. If something is in an art gallery and people are looking at it, does that make it art? Could it be a case of 'the Emperor's New Clothes', rather than something inherent in the art itself?

Consider aesthetic beauty versus religious beauty. Are they different? If so, on what criteria do we assess beauty? The concept of beauty is culturally dependent but beauty in all cultures gives us a pleasurable feeling after perceiving it.

The human face is considered more beautiful if it is symmetrical but styles of human beauty change over time and place. Our perception of beauty may be embedded in science – it may be that we gained evolutionary advantage by mating with more 'beautiful' people.

Is putting a goldfish in a blender 'art'? Is it wrong? Can immoral art be good art?

▲ Peter Paul Rubens: *Venus at a mirror*
Venus was a Roman goddess of love. Rubens was Flemish Baroque artist (1577–1640) who painted full-figured woman. Do you find this to be your ideal of beauty?

Find out more

You can read the story of the Emperor's New Clothes here: http://www.andersen.sdu.dk/vaerk/hersholt/TheEmperorsNewClothes_e.html

▲ This ancient pot is beautiful to some people. Do you think it was designed to be an object of beauty, or simply an object of use?

▲ The Golden Ratio (1:1.6) is found in many examples in the natural and human-made world and is thought to be aesthetically pleasing to humans. Why?

The idea of universal morality

Many philosophers of the Axial Age (such as Lao Tzu and Zoroaster) saw good and evil in a perpetual struggle on Earth.

The duality of good and bad appears in many religious and other texts. In the Bible, Adam and Eve disobey God and eat an apple and so become corrupted and evil. After that act, all humans were born sinful and the idea of punishing the physical body developed. Early Christian **ascetics** called stylites lived on top of pillars and martyrs were burned at stakes for their beliefs. Hair shirts, deprivation, and celibacy have all been seen as ways to become better by resisting 'evil' human instincts.

> In *The Red Queen* (1994), Matt Ridley argues that reciprocity is an advantage and so altruism — helping others — always has a common interest.

Many Axial thinkers thought that humans are naturally 'good'. Confucius wanted the state to liberate humans to reach their potential. Some Ancient Greek societies allowed citizens, regardless of their degree of education, to have a voice in running the state.

▲ An early Christian stylite living on a pillar

Others, such as Hsun Ch'ing (mid-3rd century BC) thought the opposite — that humans are naturally violent and selfish and it is civilization and laws that moderate that behaviour.

The degree of control modern-day states exert over their people often depends on their view of human morality. It could be said that moral pessimism is demonstrated by conservatives who want to regulate the state to control us and optimism by socialists who believe that human nature is basically good.

One problem with the optimistic view is that it involves what we *ought* to do. We cannot derive ethical rules from facts. Ethics seem not to be rational but are in fact about doing what *seems* right through our use of intuition.

Do you think that science is value free, making no moral judgments? What is it that causes us to feel that something is right or wrong?

Culture is one answer to this question. Cannibalism is considered wrong in most cultures but in some it is traditional to eat a part of your dead ancestor. Moral truth may not be an absolute but to say it is all relative, that it depends on your cultural background, leads to other difficulties in which 'anything goes'.

Religions provide ready-made value systems on questions of morality. For a believer of one of the three religions of the Old Testament — Judaism, Christianity and Islam — morality is based on God's commandments. Ethical values are absolutes and there is little relativity. But are things good or bad because God commands that they are (for example, don't steal) or does God command things because they are good (it is wrong to steal so God demands that we do not)?

Without belief in God or gods determining our moral value systems, morality may be a result of our capacity to share the feelings of others — empathy. In that case, it is emotion that decides if something is right or wrong and reason that then provides our motives. So we need both sentiment and reason to construct morality.

Jeremy Bentham (1794–1832) based morality on whether our actions increase or decrease human well-being. If they increase well-being for most, the actions are good; if they decrease it for most, they are bad. This is **utilitarianism**.

> *The greatest happiness for the greatest number.*
> Jeremy Bentham, British philosopher, 1748–1832

Bentham wrote that it is best to maximize pleasure. John Stuart Mill modified this and tried to categorize types of pleasure, measuring some as more valuable than others. For Mill, pleasures of an intellectual and aesthetic nature are more valuable than physical ones.

This rule of utilitarianism allows us to make rational decisions about the least bad choice. A well-known ethical dilemma which discusses this is the '**Trolley Problem**'.

Imagine there is a runaway trolley careering down a railway track. Ahead, on the track, there are five people who are unable to move. The trolley is headed straight for them. You are standing some distance off, next to a lever. If you pull this lever, the trolley will switch to a different set of tracks. On that track, there is one person, also unable to move. You have two options – if you do nothing, the trolley will kill the five people on the main track. If you pull the lever to divert the trolley onto the side track, it will kill one person.

 Which is the correct choice?

▲ An example of the trolley problem. What do you do? How do you decide?

The least bad option is used to justify many actions where the alternative would harm more people. Dropping atom bombs on Hiroshima and Nagasaki killed over 200,000 people. It was argued that more lives than that were saved because that action brought about a faster surrender by the Japanese to the Allies in the Second World War. How do you think the decision was made?

> *Reason is, and ought only to be the slave of the passions and can never pretend to any other office than to serve and obey them.*
>
> David Hume, Scottish philosopher, 1711–76, *Treatise of Human Nature* (1739)

David Hume believed that reason and rationality should be guided by 'the passions'. Others, led by the English philosopher R M Hare, feel that using emotion to define why something is right or wrong misses the use of rational argument and that morals should be guiding our actions – there should be laws such as 'do not kill' which are universal.

The **Golden Rule** of 'do as you would be done by' is found in most religions and could be seen as a moral law. But is the Golden Rule enough of a moral code to live by?

> *One should always treat others as they themselves wish to be treated.*
>
> Hinduism: 3200 BC, From the Hitopadesa

> *What you do not want done to yourself, do not do to others.*
>
> Confucianism: 557 BC, From the Analects 15:23

> *Hurt not others with that which pains yourself.*
>
> Buddhism: 560 BC, From the Udanavarga 5:18

> *Thou shalt love thy neighbour as thyself.*
>
> Judaism: 1300 BC, Old Testament, Leviticus 19:18

> *Whatsoever ye would that others should do to you, do ye even so to them.*
>
> Christianity: 30 CE, King James Bible, 7:12

> *Hurt no one so that no one may hurt you.*
>
> Islam: Prophet Muhammad's last sermon 630 CE

For Emmanuel Kant, morality was a matter of what he called 'categorical imperatives' – absolute rules which he said were the fundamentals of morality. One of these is never to lie because we must respect others as we would want them to respect us, and lying is a form of disrespect. Kant would encourage us always to tell the truth, whatever the consequences.

Should I try to change the world?

Yes!

'Liberty will Roll all the Tyrants of the Universe in the Dust'

Jean-Paul Marat, *L'Ami du Peuple*, 1791

Across Europe and America in the eighteenth century, it suddenly seemed possible to kick out kings and unelected rulers, and replace them with new — perhaps better — forms of government. The success of the American and French Revolutions made many philosophers and politicians think that we all had the right to guard our liberty by overthrowing governments when they became tyrannical or started to behave unjustly. After all, these thinkers argued, what right did kings have to tell us what to do? The answer, they said, was that kings had no right, so they could be overthrown. The idea that we have the right to change the government's actions (or even overthrow it entirely) has remained popular ever since.

No!

'The measure of Good and Evil actions is the Civil Law'

Thomas Hobbes, *Leviathan*, 1651

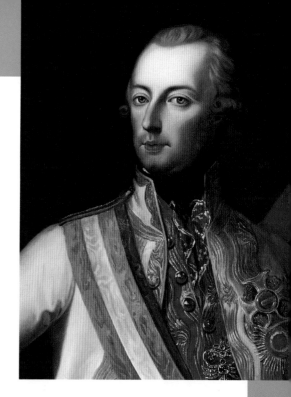

The problem with liberty is that people don't know what's best for them.

This, in a nutshell, is what authoritarian thinkers and rulers have thought for at least 2,500 years. The ancient Greek philosopher Plato argued that most of us are not well informed enough to know what is best for our countries, and argued that we should give up government to wise 'philosopher kings'. Writing after the slaughter of the English Civil War, another philosopher, Thomas Hobbes, argued that the only way of avoiding a life that was 'nasty, brutish and short,' was to give up all government power to a sovereign whose will could never be challenged, because, if it was, anarchy and suffering would follow. Kings and emperors like Joseph II of Austria (above) picked up on Hobbes' ideas and enthusiastically prevented anyone else from having any say in government. Rulers like Joseph weren't evil (Joseph even invested royal money in creating beautiful public parks), but they did absolutely deny that their people had the right to revolt.

In other words...

Should we have the right to protest and even overthrow our governments, at the risk of this leading to violent revolution?

Or...

Should we permanently give up our right to have a say in government, so we will always avoid the horrors of violence, revolution and civil war?

'I believe in cutting off heads.'

Jean-Paul Marat, author of both of the quotations on this page, had a very clear idea of liberty and of the responsibilities all citizens had. Writing in the midst of the French Revolution (1789–94), Marat constantly urged the ordinary people of Paris to take government into their own hands. The king, he argued, had shown that he was corrupt and a tyrant. Elected politicians had proved to be complete failures, too. So there was only one option: the people had to take power into their own hands, executing everyone who stood in their way. Marat believed that all rulers – kings or prime ministers – would eventually be corrupted, and argued that their decisions should always be subject to approval by the people themselves. The reason for Marat's remarkable violence is that he believed that rulers were *so* corrupt that there was no other option other than to kill them outright. For Marat, liberty was worth the price of a few hundred (or thousand) politicians' deaths.

'Five or six hundred heads would have guaranteed your freedom and happiness but a false humanity has restrained your arms and stopped your blows. If you don't strike now, millions of your brothers will die, your enemies will triumph and your blood will flood the streets. They'll slit your throats without mercy and disembowel your wives. And their bloody hands will rip out your children's entrails to erase your love of liberty forever.'

Unfortunately for Marat, some of his enemies took his advice to take power into their own hands more literally than others. Charlotte Corday, an enemy of his, took the opportunity to stab him to death as he worked in his bath-tub, in 1793.

James Wilson:
The American alternative

> 'Let a state be considered as subordinate to the people: But let everything else be subordinate to the state.'

As both a distinguished politician and judge, James Wilson could have been expected to disagree with Marat's revolutionary enthusiasm: for Wilson, we all had to obey the law and generally behave ourselves. But, as one of the leaders of the American War of Independence and signer of the Declaration of Independence , Wilson did believe in *some* forms of Revolution – in his case, removing the authority of the English king from America. So how did he manage to be both a believer in the power of government, *and* a committed revolutionary?

Yes to revolution – sometimes...

Wilson believed that sometimes, very occasionally, it was right to protest and overthrow your government. But this wasn't something a crowd of people could just *decide* to do. In order to have a 'legitimate' revolution, leaders or politicians had to make a careful survey of the views of the people in their area, and work out whether a majority of them wanted a violent change of government. If they did, then there had to be a very clear and well worked-out reason why other forms of trying to change things would not work. And the revolution had to be led throughout by sensible and educated people (like him). It was only when all these conditions had been fulfilled that a political system could be overthrown. Yes, you could change the world dramatically – but only by being very careful about it.

But yes to a strong government, too...

Once a revolution had taken place, however, the people needed to be ruled effectively. Permanent revolution (the sort of thing Marat seemed to be arguing for) was not a good thing. Wilson believed that, once the Revolution was over, a new government needed to be set up that was basically democratic. Once people had the vote and were able to choose their politicians, this would remove the need for any future revolution. A political system based on the idea of the 'sovereignty of the people' (a term Wilson by-and-large invented) would stabilize government in the long run, and remove any need for violent revolt.

Was Wilson right?

131

'During the time men live **without a common power** to keep them all in awe, they are in that condition which is called **war;** and such a war, as is of every man, against every man. In such condition, there is no place for industry; because the fruit thereof is uncertain: and consequently no culture of the earth; no navigation, nor use of the commodities that may be imported by sea; no commodious building; no instruments of moving, and removing, such things as require much force; no knowledge of the face of the earth; no account of time; no arts; no letters; no society; and which is worst of all, continual fear, and danger of violent death; **and the life of man, solitary, poor, nasty, brutish, and short.'**

Thomas Hobbes

Thomas Hobbes had a very dim view of humanity. In Hobbes' view, a society without a strong government would descend, sooner or later, into chaos and war in which, in his famous phrase, life would be 'solitary, poor, nasty, brutish, and short.' It's a safe bet that none of us want to live that sort of life, so the only alternative, in Hobbes' view, is to give up, forever, all our political rights to an all-powerful 'sovereign', or ruler. This ruler would then be unable to do wrong, because nobody would be allowed to challenge them. This is a difficult concept for many modern people to understand, since most of us have some understanding of human rights. But for Hobbes, we would have to give up all our rights to the sovereign in return for them preventing us from lapsing into civil war. Hobbes was strongly influenced in this view by the fact that he lived through the destruction of the English Civil War in the mid-seventeenth century, and wanted to prevent such a traumatic experience from ever happening again. As the life of Marat shows, however, Hobbes was not successful.

Hobbes argued that, in his ideal world, the sovereign would act on behalf of the people he ruled, even if the people didn't agree with him. Ideally, perhaps, the sovereign would act in the best interests of his people. In real life, rulers like this have existed. Joseph II of Austria (who also ruled an enormous chunk of central Europe, and large portions of Germany and Italy) took the role of emperor extremely seriously. He listened to advice remarkably infrequently, and took an incredibly detailed interest in all government matters, including whether the street-lights in Vienna were working correctly. But historians have seen Joseph's autocratic rule as planting the seeds of the Austrian Empire's downfall in 1918: the people of his empire simply did not like him meddling in their lives.

So, should I try to change the world, or not?

According to the philosophers, you have three options.

1

You must! At all times!

This would be Marat's view. Unless we are all constantly on our guard against tyrants and corrupt rulers, we will be tricked into giving up our liberty, possibly forever. We must not be sentimental in guarding our liberty, because it's too important for that. So, if we need to be violent, we should be. Executing the enemies of liberty must be a priority. The revolution should last for as long as it needs to.

2

You can, via the political system.

This would be Wilson's view. Although at certain times revolutions might be necessary, if you live in a proper democracy, they should not be. In a democracy, trust in your politicians and use your right to vote if you don't like them. Their authority comes from the people, so they ought to be responsive to the people's wishes.

3

Never!

This would be Hobbes' view. The danger of revolution or violent change is *always* too great to justify an attempt to change the world. Revolution and civil war is so horrible that it must be avoided at all costs. This means giving up all our rights to the sovereign, who may or may not be a good ruler. But it doesn't matter, because even if he's terrible, his rule is better than war.

The idea of a superior human race or superior nation

Early humans probably saw themselves as just another animal to eat or be eaten. But long before the biblical story in which God created man in his own image and gave him dominion over the other animals was written, some saw humans as superior to other animals.

> *For that some should rule and others be ruled is a thing not only necessary, but expedient; from the hour of their birth, some are marked out for subjection, others for rule...*
>
> *And indeed the use made of slaves and of tame animals is not very different; for both with their bodies minister to the needs of life.*
>
> Aristotle, Greek philosopher, 384 BC–322 BC

> *Man has spirits, life and perception, and in addition the sense of justice; therefore he is the noblest of living things.*
>
> Hsun Tzu (Xunzi), Chinese philosopher, 312–230 BC

Taking the other view were **Pythagoras**, who taught that all things that are born with life ought to be treated as kindred, and **Mahivara Vardamana**, who thought that the universality of souls meant that we should treat animals with special respect.

This dilemma has not gone away. Does our superiority in being able to shape our environment mean we have lordship or stewardship over animals? To what extent can humans exploit animals? Is there a limit?

Campaigners against animal testing cite the unnecessary suffering of the animals and say that the drugs and procedures can be tested in other ways. If the animals are conscious and suffer pain, is it wrong to inflict pain upon them or is it justified if there is a greater good such as curing cancer? How do we know if animals suffer pain in the same way as we do? (In fact, how do I know that you feel pain as I do?) Should we only experiment on animals less like us – so not primates or mammals? But where do we draw the line? Can fish or reptiles feel pain?

Animal rights movements are not new. Bentham wrote about them in 1788 and the Jain code of conduct involves doing your best not to harm any other living creature. In the main, humans have exploited animals as a source of food, clothing, and labour but without causing unnecessary suffering.

Do we exhibit 'species-ism' in not respecting the rights of other animals?

What about the view that some humans are superior to others?

During the time of the Zhou dynasty, the Chinese named their country 'Middle Kingdom'. The people of the rest of the world were thought of as barbarians and depicted at the edges of Chinese maps.

Japan was traditionally subservient to China, its huge neighbour, but the advent of Buddhism and pragmatic state-building led to a belief from 1890s onwards that the emperor of Japan was the senior descendant of the sun goddess and all Japanese people are descended from her too.

Like Japan after Chinese rule, it was Germany's suffering after conquest by France and Russia in the early 19th century that led to a nationalist reaction. The Volksgeist (spirit of the nation) was seen as good and civilizing and Germany was seen as the development of the Greek and Roman spirit. But how to define 'Germany'? If it was based on those who spoke the German language, then 'Germany' could cross national boundaries as long as there were people there who spoke German, even if they were in a minority. It was this form of nationalism that led to the world wars of the 20th century.

▲ Emperor Hirohito of Japan at his enthronement in 1928. The imperial line dates back to 660 BC.

The British Empire (late 16th to 20th century) was, at its peak, the largest empire in the history of civilization with 20 per cent of the world's population living within its colonies and other territories. It developed through the Age of Discovery (15th and 16th centuries) when European powers (particularly Spain, Portugal, and Britain) sent explorers across the oceans and claimed the lands they found for their own nations. After the Second World War, most colonies gained independence from Britain and established their own governments.

Find out more

The Course of German History, AJP Taylor, 1945

These examples are instances where patriotism has thrived. Patriotism is a love of your homeland and its culture. Nationalism is a type of patriotism in which the nation is seen as a homogenous group. That may be based on cultural, religious, or ethnic criteria. There have been instances throughout history where nationalism has developed into something more sinister and destructive.

The idea of human rights

Historically, there has been a balance between state and people. The people are subjects of the state. The state provides them with some form of protection and, in exchange, demands that they give up certain individual rights. Subjects (or citizens) have to obey the laws of the state and pay their taxes. But what if the state demands too much of their citizens?

Are there some rights that are too important for a state to overrule? How do we know what these are?

In both France and America, revolutionaries demanded that the fundamental rights be codified. 'Liberté, Égalité, Fraternité ou la mort' (Liberty, Equality, Fraternity or death) was a slogan of the French Revolution, although 'ou la mort' was later dropped.

Similarly the right to 'Life, liberty and the pursuit of happiness' was at the heart of the 1776 American Declaration of Independence.

In both cases, the interpretation of these rights was vague. In America, slaves and their descendants were denied human rights for a long time and capital punishment still exists in 31 states.

Liberté • Égalité • Fraternité

RÉPUBLIQUE FRANÇAISE

The United Nations Declaration of Human Rights (1948) was created after the Second World War and was the first worldwide statement of rights to which all humans are entitled.

Find out more

You can read the United Nations Declaration of Human Rights here: http://www.un.org/en/documents/udhr/index.shtml.

Ideas about society

The idea of rules and laws

Banning certain foodstuffs because they are taboo (forbidden) is common in many societies. A ban could be the result of food hygiene, implemented when it became clear that eating mouldy food made you ill or even killed you. Or perhaps the most valued foods are banned to certain people. However, studies show that there are few rational and physical explanations for banned foods within various religions. Perhaps food taboos are more about uniting those who respect them and reinforcing a sense of shared identity.

Cannibalism is carried out by some species. In our own species, eating other people could be viewed as a legitimate method of survival if food is scarce but most societies ban it.

Incest is prohibited in most societies but the extent varies. In ancient Egypt, pharaohs married their daughters. In many royal families, marriages between cousins are the norm. Some suggest that children whose parents have close family ties have more hereditary defects but that is not usually the case. It seems that the taboo incest is not the result of biological rules but societal ones.

In *The Elementary Structures of Kinship* (1949), The French anthropologist Claude Levi-Strauss argued that exchanging women across family groups made the society stronger as bonds were made between unrelated families and created mutual obligations. For a social species, this expansion of strong groups was a good thing.

The idea of the state

The state is the political way of gathering a society together when it gets too big for the family, tribe, or village. Before agriculture allowed hunter-gatherers to settle down and become farmers, statehood was not possible. Overpopulation and demand for limited resources, be it water, food, or land, meant that the institutions that monitored how much we each took became stronger as disputes multiplied.

Some nomadic communities today (such as Aboriginals in Australia and African nomad tribes) do not recognize nation states as sedentary peoples do.

The state has to have a leader just as the family, tribe, or village has one, often the father or strongest/cleverest/oldest man. Kings fulfilled this role in most early states and still do in many. Inherited power was and is strong as the potential inheritors expect to receive their due and the status quo is supported by those who gain from it.

Even benign states hold tyranny over some citizens as it is inevitable that we give up freedoms to become citizens of the state. The balance between individual and state fluctuates depending on the system and the perceived threat to the state.

It is generally agreed that the state's purpose is to make its citizens good through virtue or happiness or both. As long as a ruler is bound by the laws of the state and these laws are ethical, things should work. But Macchiavelli's *The Prince* (1513) suggested that you could be politically successful by lying, cheating, and being unjust. In short, by having no morality. The ruler's one aim was to stay in power and everything else was secondary. Such ruthlessness led to the doctrine of **realpolitik** in which the state serves itself and is not subject to moral laws. Machiavelli's book could be viewed as hugely ironic, but this has been missed by most readers who have taken it seriously and acted accordingly.

? Can you think of leaders, past or present, who appear to have no morality or take a different view of morality to your own?

Various versions of the state have been tried over the centuries, some more successfully than others.

In *The Republic*, Plato thought he could design a perfect society which had a benevolent ruling class. In the book, Socrates, the main character, describes this group – the Guardians or philosopher-kings – who would be self-elected intellectuals who gained their position through heredity and education and who were selfless and 'god-like' in their ability to know what was good for the citizens.

Justice in *The Republic* is the compromise made by the state.

The people (the plebs) have to be controlled by the Guardians because they do not know what is best for them, being less educated than the Guardians. This is illustrated famously in Plato's allegory of the cave within the book.

The idea of the Guardians finds echoes in aristocracies, elites, and self-appointed tyrants who all justify their rule because 'they know best'. To maintain the state in this form, Plato has to bring in censorship, collectivism and sharing of goods, militarism, austerity, rigid class structure, and dictatorship. We do not have to look far to see these aspects in states today.

▲ Machavelli

How can we judge if humans are naturally good or bad or neither?

This question has been fundamental to paths taken by states. If we are naturally good 'noble savages' who live by natural justice and the rule of reason, then states should give us freedoms. But if we are naturally bad, 'not noble but savage savages' in which 'the life of man is poor, nasty, brutish and short', as in Thomas Hobbes' *Leviathan* (1651), then the state should take control of our lives for our own good (see Big Questions p132). The later theory tends to have prevailed and citizens give up all rights except that of self-preservation to the state because only then can the weak survive. This has ramifications for relationships between states. So wars to take over territory, goods or peoples are justified and peace treaties are needed to stop that happening.

▲ Plato's allegory of the cave

The idea of a perfect state and perfect society within it has been long debated. The book *Utopia* (Thomas More, 1561) describes a perfect island state in the middle of the Atlantic. (Utopia is Greek for 'no place'.)

Find out more

- *Lord of the Flies*, William Golding, 1954
- *The Songlines*, Bruce Chatwin, 1986

The idea of the social contract

Citizens give up some of their rights to be protected by the state and the state agrees to protect its citizens through its laws. The balance between the rights that the citizens keep and those they give up is part of the social contract and varies from state to state and between different types of state system.

Rights can be classified into natural and legal rights.

> ..*the life of man, solitary, poor, nasty, brutish, and short.*
>
> Thomas Hobbes, English philosopher, 1588–1679, *Leviathan*, 1651
>
> Writing about a time of civil war in England, Hobbes thought that only the state can ensure peace through its strength.

> In *A Theory of Justice* (1971) John Rawls described justice as fairness in which there should be a 'veil of ignorance' behind which we decide the principles of justice and in which: *'no one knows his place in society, his class position or social status, nor does he know his fortune in the distribution of natural assets and abilities, his intelligence, strength, and the like.'*
>
> John Rawls, American philosopher, 1921–2002

▲ Sir Thomas More and his idea of
▼ Utopia

The idea of democracy

Aristotle and Plato condemned democracy. While the ancient Greeks and French Revolutionaries used the word, neither Greece nor France were democracies in the sense of the American one. In Greece, it was a small elite who made decisions. In France, it was not until 1848 that male suffrage (the vote) was granted. In America in the late 18th century universal suffrage (the right to vote for all adults) took hold – although even then only for white males. The ability to make laws or to elect representatives to make laws means political self-determination and means that we can oust leaders through elections rather than through revolution or civil war. Democracy brings human liberties and responsibilities and also the belief that all are equal before the law.

In *Democracy in America* (1835) the French political thinker and historian Alexis de Tocqueville envisaged: 'a society which all, regarding the law as their work, would love and submit to it without trouble'.

When the known world was smaller than it is today, total control of it seemed possible. The Roman, Egyptian, Chinese Shang dynasty, and Mongol empires were super-states. Covering massive areas and inhabited by millions of citizens, the state controlled by force and trade. Common religious practices helped bind citizens as did a common coinage but, in the end, all these universal states failed. It seems odd that we still seek world government in some form, such as the United Nations, with its ideal for peace and harmony, when history has shown it has not yet worked. The current debate over the EU (a trade-driven super-state) shows how difficult it is to reconcile national and sub-national desires.

The idea of a just war

Can wars be justified? There is a set of conditions generally agreed to justify starting a war. These are:

- Just cause – that could be in self-defence if another country invades your own or to help a country under attack.

- Right intention – that military action will further the just cause, to right the wrong.

- By proper authority – the decision to take up arms must be made by the state acting on behalf of the people.

- As a last resort – other peaceful options should first be exhausted.

- Reasonable chance of success – but what is reasonable and what if the aggressor was going to kill you all if they won?

- Be proportional – do more good than harm; the benefit must be worth the cost.

TASK

All these conditions are open to interpretation. Consider recent wars (for example, in Afghanistan and Iraq) and hold a debate on whether the war is just or not.

Do I exist?

Obviously!

Until Descartes came along in the seventeenth century, everyone assumed that we existed. Obviously. The fact seemed so mind-blowingly obvious that it wasn't really discussed. We could see ourselves in the mirror, we could feel pain and pleasure, we could think thoughts for ourselves – and, more importantly, perhaps, all the world's main religions assumed that we do exist. So, we exist.

No you don't

You don't exist. That's because it's impossible to show once and for all that you do. There's no proof. You might *think* you exist – that you're sitting at a table reading this book, for instance – but how could you show with 100 per cent certainty that this is true? There's no experiment that could prove it. Although Descartes said that you could prove your own existence by the fact that you are able to think, this isn't actually true, according to the British philosopher A.J. Ayer (above right). Just because we know that we are thinking, this doesn't mean that there is a 'you' doing the thinking. It just shows that the thoughts are happening, not that anyone is having them. Thoughts exist. 'You' don't.

What a pointless question!

What a waste of time this question is. Although you can argue until the end of time whether you exist or not, it doesn't get you anywhere. Unless you forget about this unanswerable question, you'll be stuck thinking about it forever, and that isn't of any use to anyone. Move on. Think about something more important! This, very roughly, is the view of almost all philosophers, who prefer to answer other, apparently more useful, questions.

Yes, but...

You exist, but not in the way you might think. According to the great French philosopher René Descartes (right), you can't show that anything exists — apart from your own self. The existence of the entire world can be doubted in one way or another, but the fact you're having thoughts shows that there must be *something* (that's you) having them. This led Descartes to write the famous philosophical phrase, 'I think, therefore I am' (*cogito ergo sum* in Latin.) But the idea that you only know you exist because you think can have some worrying implications, which you can see on the next page.

Does the world exist?

It certainly does

...and we should try our best to find out about it

Some of the world's greatest philosophers and religious leaders have weighed in on this question, and reached the conclusion that our common-sense understanding of the world 'out there' is wrong. From the Buddha arguing that we'll remain unenlightened unless we let go of our instinct that the world exists as we see it, to Bishop Thomas Berkeley in the eighteenth century arguing that the world only exists so long as someone (or something) is looking at or sensing it, to the great Immanuel Kant replying only a few years later that the world as we think of it exists somehow beyond and separately from what is physically out there, philosophers have tied themselves in knots trying to answer once and for all this fundamental question.

Not in the way you probably think

It's common sense. The world exists (largely) as we perceive it using our senses – and, to argue otherwise will result in us getting nowhere and fooling ourselves about the true nature of reality.

From modern physicists trying to understand how the universe functions by doing experiments and creating complex equations, back to the ninth-century Islamic thinker Avicenna and Aristotle in 350 BC, there's a long and distinguished history of thinkers who believe the world is (by and large) how we perceive it, and that it deserves our investigation.

The big idea
I think, therefore I am

It's the most famous idea in philosophy. And it's what TOK is all about.

René Descartes was an exceptionally smart individual. He made big discoveries in maths and geometry, but his most famous statement – 'I think, therefore I am' – was a philosophical one. Surprisingly, Descartes came up with his world-changing sentence one day while he was reflecting on how much he *didn't* know. Looking back on his childhood in particular, he surprised himself by remembering how many things he believed then which now, in his retirement, he knew to be wrong (presumably, as a child he believed in the seventeenth-century equivalent of the tooth fairy, for instance). This troubled Descartes. He worried that if beliefs he once thought were certain could be shown to be totally wrong, then this could also be true for any of the views he held right now. In other words, Descartes began to doubt himself, and everything he believed. His doubt led him to the question, 'How do I know anything at all?'

The big doubt

After a bit of thinking, Descartes came to believe that there was no way he could show *for certain* that anything he knew was true. How did he come to this radical (and perhaps quite depressing) conclusion? His answer was the 'evil demon'. An evil demon, Descartes argued, *could* be controlling his (and our) thoughts, putting ideas in our heads and making us *think* that we could see, hear, and feel things that actually were not happening. Descartes didn't seriously think this demon actually existed, but he argued that it *could* exist, and that (more importantly) you could not prove for certain that it did *not* exist. So Descartes was left thinking that we could not know anything for certain. With one exception.

Cogito ergo sum

We could doubt everything, Descartes thought, except for the fact that we were doubting. If we are doubting – or thinking, in other words – then there must be something *doing* the thinking, Descartes thought. And that 'something doing the thinking' is us. If we think, we must exist. Or, another way, 'I think, therefore I am.'

Descartes on TOK…

Descartes didn't take the IB Diploma, or TOK. But when he asked the question 'What do I know?' he asked the most important question in TOK, bar none. But Descartes' answer wouldn't have got many marks in a presentation or essay. What would Descartes have thought about the ways of knowing? What would he have thought of the idea of 'shared knowledge'? Does 'I think, therefore I am' convince *you*? Does it help you to understand TOK?

Was Descartes right?

A lot of people think the statement 'I think, therefore I am' is obviously true. But it's not as simple as that. In fact, there are three big questions Descartes left unanswered...

What happens when I go to sleep?

Do you stop existing when you stop thinking? Descartes would seem to think so, but this is a very odd idea indeed.

What about things you remember?

This is related to the problem above. If the only thing you can know for certain is that 'you think', then this means that everything you remember could be false. Once again, this gives a pretty strange idea of who 'you' are. If you exist without any true memories, then you're a pretty odd person.

What is the 'I' doing the thinking?

Descartes' idea that 'I think' has annoyed many philosophers. That's because if the only thing 'you' can do is 'think', then this is a very strange idea of existence. Your idea of yourself probably includes lots of things that are much more than thinking. Your relationships with friends and family, for instance, are probably an important part of what you think 'you' are. But, according to Descartes, this doesn't count. The only 'true' thing about you, is that you can think.

So do I exist, or not?

Err.. Maybe?

Philosophers have been debating Descartes' idea ever since it was first published in 1637. They haven't reached any solid conclusions in the almost 400 years since. **Is that a problem?** *Perhaps we should just stop caring about whether we exist?* **But, on the other hand, shouldn't we be rather worried if we can't prove something so basic as our own existence?** *What do you (err...) think?*

SECTION 6
TOKOPOLIS – the game of taming TOK

What is TOKOPOLIS?

TOK is sometimes a difficult beast to tame so here is TOKOPOLIS, the tool that will help you to tame TOK!

The thing with TOK is that it is often very different from anything else that you may have come across before. Think of TOK as a lens through which we view the world. TOKOPOLIS is a way of bringing that lens into focus.

TOKOPOLIS is essentially a discussion platform; a fun way for you and your friends:

- to get together and thrash out the issues of TOK
- to work practically with WOKs and AOKs
- to recognise what is **Personal Knowledge** and what is **Shared Knowledge** and the role both play in looking at the world through the TOK lens

You may, or may not, have heard of the **VAK** way of defining learning styles. There are three main ways through which receive information from the world around us:

- through our eyes – this is **Visual** learning
- through our ears – this is **Auditory** learning
- through our sense of movement and touch – this is **Kinaesthetic** learning

We all learn in different ways and, in most people, one of these ways of learning is dominant. You probably have friends who learn best through seeing pictures or writing notes – they learn visually. Some talk to themselves (not just the mad ones!) and listen to others to soak up information audibly. There are others (maybe you) who need to move or to do to learn, and for whom sitting still in class for most of the day is a bit of a nightmare. This final group are likely to be the kinaesthetic learners

For you kinaesthetic learners, who do best when moving or touching, TOK can be rather daunting. Never fear, help is at hand! TOKOPOLIS!!! Making and using this practical forum for discussion should help you 'get' TOK.

Even if you think your dominant learning style is as a visual or auditory learner, sometimes it helps to picture abstract concepts as concrete things. TOKOPOLIS gives you the framework in which you can explore TOK, allowing you to take control of TOK, instead of vice versa!

You can use TOKOPOLIS to:

- discuss **Big Questions**
- prepare **TOK Presentations**
- prepare **TOK Essays**
- understand **Contemporary Issues** – try using it to discuss today's news headlines

Step 1 – create your WOKs

WOKS are the creatures that represent the **ways of knowing** – the ways in which we perceive, think about, and make sense of the world. The **WOKS** have different characteristics, different strengths and different personalities. The usefulness of an individual **WOK** will depend on the question under discussion.

Your **WOKS** can be made of anything you like – drawn on card and cut out, made of clay or Plasticine, knitted …… just make them memorable for you so that one glance reminds you which **WOK** they are. The table on the next page shows our WOKS, some of which are, admittedly, a bit desperate – maybe we should have knitted them!

WOK	NAME	CHARACTERISTICS	STRENGTHS	WEAKNESSES
Language	LANGWOK	■ Talks a lot ■ Careful with words ■ Likes to be social.	■ Will ensure discussion. ■ Can be useful to establish the authenticity of many perspectives.	■ Not good when quiet reflection is needed. ■ May be pedantic. ■ Can cause misunderstandings
Sense perception	PERCEWOK	■ Makes sense of the world through the five senses(sight, hearing, touch, taste and smell)	■ Uses facts. ■ Works in the moment. ■ Shared by almost all human beings, regardless of race or religion.	■ Subjective perspective. ■ May struggle to effectively share experiences.
Emotion	EMOWOK	■ Interprets the world through feelings ■ Often clearly displays reactions.	■ Compassionate. ■ Works well to unite groups through shared experiences.	■ Prone to being subjective. ■ Can obstruct logical arguments. ■ May inflame delicate situations.
Reason	REASOWOK	■ Looks at all sides of a question ■ Uses logic to approach and solve problems.	■ Objective perspective. ■ Uses evidence to support arguments.	■ May clash with Emowok. ■ May lack understanding of illogical paradigms. ■ May become frustrated if a situation can't be understood quickly.

WOK	NAME	CHARACTERISTICS	STRENGTHS	WEAKNESSES
Imagination	IMAGIWOK	■ Looks at the world in terms of what "could be" rather than what is. ■ Little time for facts, much more focus on alternative scenarios.	■ Visionary. ■ Able to introduce alternative scenarios and solutions.	■ May clash with Reasowok. ■ May produce impossible suggestions. ■ May become frustrated by overly practical or pragmatic approaches.
Faith	FAITHWOK	■ Operates from the perspective of religious and non-religious belief systems.	■ Will stand by beliefs and treat all knowledge questions within the same framework.	■ May approach knowledge questions from very limited perspective. ■ May be an inflammatory presence in some scenarios. ■ May clash with Reowok and Perwok.
Intuition	INTUWOK	■ Acts and reacts according to what *feels* right.	■ May have a knack of being able to identify courses of action without much discussion	■ May seem to be quite illogical at times. Often unable to produce tangible evidence for actions and arguments.
Memory	MEMOWOK	■ Interprets the world and knowledge questions based on what has happened before.	■ Will have a good understanding of history, both personal and shared.	■ Arguments may be overly subjective. ■ May be ignored by other WOKs.

Step 2 – map out the AOK districts

Now that you have your WOKS, it's time to create your TOK world, your TOKOPOLIS!

Each area in your TOKOPOLIS represents an Area of Knowledge (**AOK**). **AOKs** are areas where your WOKS will meet to discuss the **Knowledge Questions**. **AOKS** may be continents, countries, cities, whatever works for the **Knowledge Question** under discussion.

Decide on the names of **your AOK** districts. We have chosen actual places, but TOKOPOLIS is **your world**, so feel free to make up your own places. Give your **AOKS** names (real or imaginary) and descriptions that will help you to shape your arguments. We have based our TOKOPOLIS on the whole world, but you could use any city, town, or country, or you could invent a new world of your own. This really is up to you, it's your game, it's your world, it's your TOKOPOLIS!

Iraq

AOK: mathematics

The earliest evidence of Mathematics can be traced back to the Babylonian civilization of Mesopotamia, or Iraq as we know it today. Amongst other things Mathematics was developed to measure plots of land and implement a system of taxation.

Suggested WOK links: Reason, Imagination, Language

Hawaii

AOK: natural sciences

Hawaii is made up of volcanoes. Each island is made up of at least one primary volcano, although many islands are composites of more than one. Amazingly people still live there. In fact **Hawaii** is the home of *Mauna Loa* the largest volcano on Earth. What better example of the power of Nature could there be?

Suggested WOK links: Reason, Perception, Language

Ethiopia

AOK: history

The African country of **Ethiopia** is where the *Ardipithecus ramidus* fossils were discovered. The *Ardipithecus ramidus* fossils are the oldest human remains to be found anywhere, which suggests that Ethiopia is the birthplace of the human race.

Suggested WOK links: Reason, Memory, Imagination, Language

Italy

AOK: the arts

The Italian city of **Florence** is home to some of the most beautiful works of art in the world. Hardly surprising when you find out that Michelangelo, Leonardo da Vinci, Dante and Boccacio all lived there at some point.

Suggested WOK links: Imagination, Emotion, Language, Perception, Faith, Memory

Switzerland

AOK: ethics

Geneva in Switzerland is home to the United Nations. A place for discussion, the UN contains enough seating for representatives of each of the World's nations.

Suggested WOK links: Reason, Language, Perception, Memory

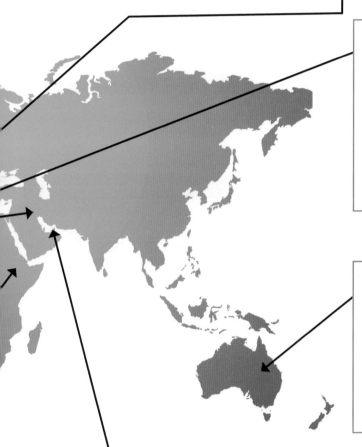

Greece

AOK: religious knowledge systems

The Parthenon in **Athens**, Greece was built between 447 BC and 432 BC. It was built as a temple to the Ancient Greek Gods, one of whom was Nike, goddess of Victory (not trainers!).

Suggested WOK links: Intuition, Faith, Emotion, Language

Australia

AOK: indigenous knowledge systems

Ayers Rock is known as *Uluru* to the Aboriginal people of Australia; it is regarded as a symbol of all creation.

Suggested AOK links: Memory, Perception, Faith, Language, Intuition

Dubai

AOK: human sciences

The world's tallest tower is in **Dubai**. The design of the 2,684-foot-tall Burj Dubai building is influenced by traditional Islamic architecture. A true feat of engineering

Suggested WOK links: Imagination, Language, Perception, Reason

As you create your world, think about how you place the AOKS – are some areas close together because they are similar or are they far apart because they are so different? For example, what benefits may there be in placing history next to ethics? Might there be a conflict if the arts is next to mathematics? Or may there be unexpected areas of collaboration? Create a TOKOPOLIS that will be of greatest benefit to the Knowledge Question under discussion.

Step 3 – you are ready to enter TOKOPOLIS

Welcome to TOKOPOLIS, a forum for discussion, debate and the sharing of paradigms!

So once you are here, what do you do?

- Look carefully at the Knowledge Question you need to discuss.
- Decide upon the most suitable AOK(s) in which to hold your discussion.
- Invite the WOKs that will be most useful in your discussion. (Choosing the WOKs could be a useful discussion in itself, the reason for inviting or excluding a particular WOK may shed new light on the subject under discussion.)
- Begin your discussion. Make notes or record the discussion as it goes along, as this will help you to understand how TOK ideas are formed and developed. Recording or making notes will also help you to format your argument for your presentation and your TOK essay.

To help you navigate the highways and byways of TOKOPOLIS, here is an example of how it could work using a TOK essay question:

> "The methods used to produce knowledge depend on the use to which it will be put."
> Discuss this statement in relation to two areas of knowledge."

Identify the knowledge question.

In this case, the knowledge question appears to be:

> Should actions be justified according to the final outcome?

Identify any AOKs which could be used.

Identify the AOKs that you want to use as the context in which to discuss the knowledge question. Record the main points of your discussion; it will help you to justify your final choices. Let's look at the AOKs which may be suitable to address this knowledge question:

- human sciences (for example, in the context of medical research)
- ethics (such as the issues surrounding medical testing)
- history (the Italian writer Machiavelli suggested that a ruler could use any means, however unscrupulous or immoral, to hold onto power)
- the arts (how do we know that the final outcome of Damian Hirst's Shark in Formaldehyde is 'art'?)

Make your choice of AOK and note the reasons for your choices.

It is important to look at both sides of the knowledge question. This example will focus on **human science** and **ethics**.

The *negative impact* of developments in **human science** may result in death, injury or unhappiness. Examples could be:

- instances of clinical trials going wrong, and causing harm (this website gives an example from the UK in 2006: http://news.bbc.co.uk/1/hi/england/london/4808836.stm)
- impressive buildings and feats of engineering which are potentially unsustainable and environmentally damaging (as argued in this article about Dubai's Burj Khalifa: http://www.guardian.co.uk/culture/2010/jan/10/burj-khalifa-dubai-skyscraper-architecture)
- examples of drugs which have had unforeseen side effects (Thalidomide was used widely throughout the 1950s and 60s, but resulted in many babies being born with deformed limbs: http://www.thalidomidetrust.org/story)

We also need to consider the *positive impact* of developments in human science. This is where you may find that you can refer to your personal knowledge in relation to things that have happened to you or people you know. For example, you may have suffered from an illness that has been treated with procedures or medicine that were developed through medical research. But are these methods **ethically** sound? What if that medical research involved animal testing?

 Find out more

Cancer research uses animal testing to develop cancer fighting drugs: http://scienceblog.cancerresearchuk. org/2011/06/21/animal-research-is-helping-us-beat-cancer/

What **ethical** issues are beginning to develop as a result of our discussion so far?

■ Is human life considered more important than the lives of animals?

■ We are all eventually going to die, so why are we investing time and money in keeping alive people who are really ill, when there are other areas of humanity that the money could be used to help?

■ To what extent are we 'playing God' by interfering with nature's course? Why is this acceptable/unacceptable?

Step 4 – choose your WOKs

Work through each WOK one-by-one in order to be able to justify your reasons in your final piece of work. You may find it useful to discuss the importance of each WOK in terms of how useful or important it is in addressing the Knowledge Question, and then rank the WOKs accordingly. This will help you to decide which WOKs to focus on. Discuss and note down your reasons for your choices.

Let's consider the sort of notes we might make for our example:

■ **imagination** – needed to promote ideas of what may be possible in order to change/address the existing position. Needed to understand what life would be without medical research.

■ **language** – needed in order to communicate ideas. Specific scientific jargon may be useful.

■ **perception** – needed to read documents, listen to other perspectives. May not be needed to present the final outcome.

■ **reason** – needed to understand the possible pitfalls and benefits.

■ **memory** – needed to draw on both personal and shared experience, as well as lessons from the past.

■ **emotion** – may become too involved, too subjective, resulting in a loss of focus. Not required for this discussion.

■ **intuition** – not needed, this discussion needs to use practical and factual argument.

■ **faith** – not needed, this discussion will need to be structured within a framework of hard evidence.

■ Chosen WOKs: imagination, language, perception, reason, memory.

Step 5 – place your WOK avatars in the relevant AOK

Imagine that initially just *two* of our WOKs, let's say Imagiwok and Reasowok, meet in Geneva. The basis of the discussion will need to be within the AOK of *Ethics* as this is the AOK represented by Geneva.

Imagiwok may present a case from a perspective of what life might be like, without medical research. This argument may raise questions around whether we have an ethical duty to preserve human life, regardless of how it is done.

In response Reasowok might argue from an existentialist perspective that, as we are going to die anyway, there is little point in trying to find a way to cure fatal diseases. At this point any member of the group may recall a time in their life when they were in hospital or receiving treatment that would not have been possible without medical research *(personal knowledge)* It would be worth researching how the treatment was developed *(shared knowledge)*.

Now let's introduce Percewok who presents an argument based upon the use of animals in medical research. Reasowok may suggest using humans instead, after all humans are animals. Reasowok may take this one step further and suggest the use of prisoners in medical research. At this point Memowok may enter the discussion and remind all the other WOKs that the Nazis experimented on humans. This is when Langwok may come in – "Nazis" is a term that will always prompt a response.

Reasowok may point out that medical trials are carried out on humans, the difference being that in today's world these trials are both voluntary and often the subjects are paid to take part.

Langwok would point out that the "voluntary"/"involuntary" position makes a world of difference within Ethics

From this the discussion will continue to grow. It may be that each member of your group contributes from the perspective of a specific WOK, or you all take turns at putting forward your argument, recognising which WOK is speaking. Also note those elements of the discussion which are personal knowledge, and which are shared knowledge.

At the end of this focussed discussion, discuss the **role** of each of your chosen WOKs within the **Knowledge Question**, in relation to the AOKs you are focussing on.

How does each WOK advance or hinder your perspective? Note the impact of adding and removing each WOK to understand what weight each WOK adds to the discussion. Do some WOKs work better in isolation or in partnership? What is the significance of this? Keep a note of how much of your discussion is **personal knowledge** and how much is **shared knowledge**. This will help you to ensure that you have developed an objective argument.

By the end of this process you (and/or your group) should have an understanding of:

- a range of aspects of the Knowledge Question
- a range of perspectives on the Knowledge Question
- the impact of the AOKs on the Knowledge Question
- the impact of the WOKs on the Knowledge Question
- how to approach your essay/presentation

That's it – TOKOPOLIS is yours! Be a kind and beneficent ruler and remember:
"With great power, comes great responsibility." (Voltaire .*Œuvres de Voltaire*, 1832, via Spiderman's Uncle Ben)

OXFORD
UNIVERSITY PRESS

Great Clarendon Street, Oxford OX2 6DP

Oxford University Press is a department of the University of Oxford.
It furthers the University's objective of excellence in research,
scholarship, and education by publishing worldwide in

Oxford   New York

Auckland Cape Town Dar es Salaam Hong Kong Karachi
Kuala Lumpur Madrid Melbourne Mexico City Nairobi
New Delhi Shanghai Taipei Toronto

With offices in

Argentina Austria Brazil Chile Czech Republic France Greece
Guatemala Hungary Italy Japan Poland Portugal Singapore
South Korea Switzerland Thailand Turkey Ukraine Vietnam

Oxford is a registered trade mark of Oxford University Press
in the UK and in certain other countries

© Oxford University Press 2013

The moral rights of the author have been asserted

Database right Oxford University Press (maker)

First published 2013

British Library Cataloguing in Publication Data

Data available

ISBN: 978-0-19-912974-4

10 9 8 7 6 5 4 3

Printed in Great Britain

Paper used in the production of this book is a natural, recyclable product made
from wood grown in sustainable forests. The manufacturing process conforms
to the environmental regulations of the country of origin

MIX
Paper from
responsible sources
FSC® C007785

Acknowledgments

The publisher would like to thank the following for their kind permission to
reproduce photographs:

p4: Goodluz /Shutterstock; **p5:** Michael Leunig; **p7:** pockygallery /Shutterstock;
p12: lesniewski/Fotolia; **p12:** Robert Adrian Hillman /Shutterstock; **p12:**
Nicemonkey/ Shutterstock; **p12:** Nicemonkey /Shutterstock; **p13:** Look and
Learn/Bridgemanart Library; **p15:** feiyuezhangjie/Shutterstock; **p15:** Theophile
Emmanuel (1821-86)/ Josef Mensing Gallery, Hamm-Rhynern, Germany /
Getty Images; **p19:** Michael Leunig; **p20:** TonLammerts/Shutterstock; **p21:**
UniversalImagesGroup/Getty Images; **p25:** Mike Kemp/RubberBall/OUP;
p25: Fuse/OUP; **p26:** Everett Collection/Rex Features; **p28:** Rosli Othman /
Shutterstock; **p31:** Daniel Padavona/Shutterstock; **p32:** Dan Piraro; **p37:** AFP/
Getty Images; **p40-41:** ama54/Shutterstock; **p40:** Dragon Images/Shutterstock/
OUP; **p41:** Photodisc/OUP; **p46:** Sidney Harris; **p52:** Ray Tang/Rex Features;
p55: Photo Researchers RM/Getty Images; **p56:** Gavran333/ Shutterstock;
p56: John M. Heller/Getty Images Entertainment/Getty Images; **p57:** Panos
Karas/Shutterstock; **p57:** kosam /Shutterstock; **p57:** Imagebank; **p62:**
UniversalImagesGroup/Getty Images; **p66:** Temych/Shutterstock; **p68:** Warner
Br/Everett/Rex Features; **p73:** Chianuri/OUP; **p78:** Olga_i/Shutterstock; **p78:**
Imagebank; **p79:** Apic/Hulton Archive/Getty Images; **p80:** Steve Pyke/Premium
Archive/Getty Images; **p80:** Hulton Archive/Getty Images; **p81:** Michelangelo
Buonarroti/The Bridgeman Art Library/Getty Images; **p81:** Thinkstock/OUP; **p82:**
Omikron Omikron/Photo Researchers /Getty Images; **p83:** London School of
economics and political science; **p83:** David McGlynn/OUP; **p91:** getty images
entertainment/Getty images; **p98:** Alinari/Rex Features; **p99:** Imagebank; **p100:**
Gallo Images/Getty Images; **p100:** Kamira/Shutterstock; **p100:** Imagebank;
p101: 3D Joe and Max/Rex Features; **p102:** De Agostini/Getty Images; **p105:**
Georgios Kollidas/Shutterstock; **p106:** Kristopher Grunert/Corbis/OUP; **p107:**
Robert Hoetink/Shutterstock; **p107:** Marc van Vuren/Shutterstock; **p107:** Jose
Ignacio Soto/Shutterstock; **p108:** BasPhoto/Fotolia; **p109:** Geoffrey Robinson/
Rex Features; **p109:** ella1977/Shutterstock; **p110:** Italian ministry of culture;
p110: yienkeat/ Shutterstock; **p111:** Gareth Boden/OUP; **p111:** LAMB/OUP;
p111: Digital Vision/ OUP; **p112:** Dragon News/Rex Features; **p113:** Paul
Fleet/Shutterstock; **p113:** Schildkrötenfossil/Fotolia; **p114:** Gabe Palmer/OUP;
p115: Popperfoto/Getty Images; **p115:** RSA/Cognitive Media; **p116:** Comstock/
OUP; **p116:** De Agostini/Getty Images; **p116:** SuperStock/Glow Images; **p117:**
Jolyon Troscianke; **p118:** Stephen Gibson/ Shutterstock; **p119:** Science Photo
Library; **p119:** Theodore Gericault/The Bridgeman Art Library/Getty Images;
p120: vasabii/Shutterstock; **p122:** Robert Harding/Glow Images; **p123:** 360b/
Shutterstock; **p124:** Peter Paul Rubens/The Bridgeman Art Library/Getty
Images; **p124:** Eusebius; **p124:** dtopal/Shutterstock; **p125:** Werner Forman/
Universal Images Group/Getty Images; **p126:** Chris Madden; **p128:** Daryl Lang/
Shutterstock; **p128:** Pedro Rufo/Shutterstock; **p128:** dinozzaver/ Shutterstock;
p128: arindambanerjee/Shutterstock; **p129:** DEA / A. DAGLI ORTI/ De Agostini/
Getty Images; **p130:** Scherl/SZ Photo/Mary Evans Picture Library; **p131:** Roman
Korotkov/Shutterstock; **p134:** Keystone/Hulton Royals Collection/Getty
Images; **p135:** the official gazette of the French Republic; **p137:** De Agostini/
Getty Images; **p137:** Mary Evans Picture Library; **p138:** Peter Paul Rubens/
The Bridgeman Art Library/Getty Images; **p139:** Oleg Zabielin/Shutterstock;
p140: Steve Pyke/Premium Archive/Getty Images; **p141:** Georgios Kollidas/
Shutterstock; **p145:** 18percentgrey /Shutterstock.

Front cover and title page: Steven Vidler/Terra/Corbis; Igor Plotnikov /
Shutterstock.

Artwork and illustrations by Q2A Media and Paul Hostetler.

We are grateful for permission to reprint extracts from the following copyright
material:

IB Diploma Programme, *Theory of Knowledge Guide* (First Assessment 2015),
copyright © International Baccalaureate Organization 2013, reprinted by
permission of the International Baccalaureate Organization.

Bassma Al Jandaly: 'Nurturing Women to Be Good Mothers', *Gulf News*, Dubai,
24.3.2012, reprinted by permission of the author and the publishers, Al Nisr
Publishing LLC.

Tim Ashley: 'Maria Callas: the greatest", *The Guardian*, 14.9.2007, copyright ©
Guardian News and Media 2007, reprinted by permission of GNM.

Noam Chomsky: *Language and Mind* (3e, Cambridge University Press, 2006),
reprinted by permission of the publishers.

Ben Goldacre: 'Serious claims belong in a serious scientific paper', *The Guardian*,
19.9.2011, copyright © Guardian News and Media 2011, reprinted by permission
of GNM.

Annie Hastwell interview with Dr Keast: 'Why do some people hate the taste of
broccoli?', *ABC Science*, 2.9.2011, www.abc.net.au, reprinted by permission of the
Australian Broadcasting Corporation.

A S Kline: translation of Virgil's *Aeneid* Book 2: The building of the Trojan Horse
published at www.poetryintranslation.com,, reprinted by permission of Tony
Kline.

Ronald Knox:"There was a young man who said "God..." and "Dear Sir: You're
astonishment's odd...", reprinted by permission of A P Watt at United Agents on
behalf of Magdalen Asquith.

Kathy Marks: 'Daring Book for Girls breaks didgeridoo taboo in Australia',
The Independent, 3.9.2008, copyright © The Independent 2008, reprinted by
permission of ESI Media/The Independent.

Alyssa Newcomb: 'Oregon Faith Healer Parents Get Probation in Son's Death' ,
ABC News, 19.9.2012, reprinted by permission of ABC News Productions.

Steven Pinker: *The Language Instinct:The New Science of Language and Mind* (Allen
Lane, 1994), copyright © Steven Pinkner 1994, reprinted by permission of
Penguin Books Ltd.

Marcel Proust: *In Search of Lost Time*: Volume 1 *The Way by Swann's* translated by
Lydia Davis (Penguin, 2002), English translation copyright © Lydia Davis 2002,
reprinted by permission of Penguin Books Ltd.

John Rawls: *A Theory of Justice* (The Belknap Press of Harvard University Press,
2005), copyright © 1971 by the President and Fellows of Harvard College,
reprinted by permission of the publishers.

Tim Walker: ''Doomsayers await the end of the world', *The Independent*,
9.12.2012, copyright © The Independent 2012, reprinted by permission of ESI
Media/The Independent.

Although we have made every effort to trace and contact all copyright holders
before publication this has not been possible in all cases. If notified, the
publisher will rectify any errors or omissions at the earliest opportunity.

Any third party use of these extracts outside of this publication. is prohibited,
and interested parties should apply directly to the copyright holders named in
each case for permission.